The Pitman Motorists' Library

The Book of the
VOLKSWAGEN

Maintenance and repair in the home garage for do-it-yourself owners, covering all models up to August 1970.

Staton Abbey, M.I.M.I.

Pitman Publishing

First published 1958
Second edition 1963
Third edition 1966
Fourth edition 1968
Reprinted 1969
Fifth edition 1971
Reprinted 1971

SIR ISAAC PITMAN AND SONS LTD
Pitman House, Parker Street, Kingsway, London, WC2B 5PB
P.O. Box 6038, Portal Street, Nairobi, Kenya

SIR ISAAC PITMAN (AUST.) PTY. LTD
Pitman House, 158 Bouverie Street, Carlton, Victoria 3053, Australia

PITMAN PUBLISHING COMPANY
P.O. Box 11231, Johannesk

PITMAN PUBLISHING
6 East 43rd Street, New York, N.Y. 10017, U.S.A.

SIR ISAAC PITMAN (CANADA) LTD
495 Wellington Street West, Toronto 135, Canada

THE COPP CLARK PUBLISHING COMPANY
517 Wellington Street West, Toronto, 135, Canada

ISBN: 0 273 31617 6

Made in Great Britain at the Pitman Press, Bath
G1—(G.4193)

Preface

In planning this book it was necessary to bear in mind two requirements of the enthusiastic owner: the various maintenance jobs are usually described rather briefly in a manufacturer's instruction book, so that it is desirable to explain in greater detail the "how and why" of each job; and, with older cars, the original instruction book may have been lost and a replacement is often unobtainable, so that a complete summary of all routine maintenance is a "must," and has accordingly been included.

In addition it is appreciated that some owners may feel that they are competent to tackle more ambitious work. For the benefit of these readers a certain amount of information has been added that would normally be covered only by a workshop manual intended for the use of service stations—but here a word of warning is necessary.

Unfortunately, for better or for worse, we must face the fact that any model is a nicely balanced compromise between efficiency and the maximum economy in production. Component designs often call for the use of special tools and jigs if major dismantling and reconditioning is to be carried out. The Volkswagen is no exception to this rule and such work is, therefore, outside the scope of this book.

The keen owner, on the other hand, need not be denied the pleasure of tuning his car and improving its roadholding.

Where certain products or accessories are specifically mentioned, they are recommended as the result of extensive practical tests, but I shall always be pleased to have further reports from readers.

A word of explanation is perhaps necessary concerning the use of the term "Transporter" in this book. This has been adopted, for the sake of brevity, to cover the wide range of vehicles other than the car, convertible and Karmann-Ghia models. These include the delivery van, Kombi (estate car), Microbus, Clipper, Pick-up, Ambulance, and also the numerous motorized caravan versions of the Kombi and Microbus or Clipper which are becoming increasingly popular.

I hope that, within the limits imposed by present-day publishing costs, the book will be of real value to all Volkswagen owners. Needless to say, every effort has been made to ensure that the information is as accurate as possible; and in this respect I must acknowledge the willing and most valuable assistance so cheerfully offered by the factory at Wolfsburg and Messrs. VW Motors, in England. Without such co-operation the production of this book would not have been possible.

St. Osyth   STATON ABBEY
Essex

Contents

Preface	iii
1. FACTS AND FIGURES	1
2. ROUTINE MAINTENANCE	28
3. ENGINE SERVICING AND TUNING	49
4. FUEL SYSTEM AND CARBURATION	58
5. THE IGNITION SYSTEM	77
6. ELECTRICAL SYSTEM AND AUXILIARIES	86
7. THE BRAKES	97
8. SUSPENSION, STEERING, AND TYRES	109
9. THE BODYWORK	119
Index	123

PUBLISHER'S NOTE. In view of the approach of metrication, advantage has been taken of the preparation of the Fifth Edition to include metric equivalents, where appropriate.

I Facts and figures

SOME of the figures given in this chapter appear elsewhere in the book, but they are repeated here, in tabular form, for ease of reference. Where a more detailed explanation is required the appropriate chapter should be consulted.

Since the introduction of the original 1200 c.c. saloon (now affectionately termed the "Beetle"), the Volkswagen range has expanded to cover a wide variety of different types of car, including saloons, estate cars (also termed variants), sports coupés, convertibles and Transporters.

Models and Type Numbers. With this proliferation of different models there is an increasing tendency to refer to groups of cars which have similar mechanical characteristics by type numbers; this is especially useful, of course, when discussing maintenance and servicing. There are four basic VW types—

Type 1 The Beetle, in saloon or convertible form, and the Karmann-Ghia coupé based on the Beetle chassis: VW1200, VW1300 and VW1500 (a 1,584 c.c. engine is available for the U.S. market only).

Type 2 Commercial vehicles: Transporter, Van, Pick-up, Kombi, Microbus, Ambulance, etc.

Type 3 The original 1500 and 1500S "notch-back" saloons, 1600 TA, T, TL fast-back, estate cars (Variants) and Karmann-Ghia coupé based on these models.

Type 4 The VW411, 411L, 411E and 411LE.

THE 1200 AND 1200A BEETLE MODELS

Engine. The overhead-valve, four-cylinder rear-mounted engine is bolted to a recessed flange on the gearbox and is rubber-mounted to ensure minimum vibration. The two pairs of cylinders are horizontally opposed. The down-draught carburettor is fitted immediately above a "hot-spot" which preheats the fuel-air mixture before combustion. The carburettor is fitted with an accelerator pump and the ignition timing is constantly adjusted by an automatic advance-and-retard mechanism.

Cooling System. Air-cooling is effected by a fan which rotates at double the crankshaft speed, drawing air through an opening in the fan housing and passing it over the cylinder cooling fins. A thermostat controls the flow of cooling air and maintains an efficient engine temperature under all operating and climatic conditions.

The oil cooler, which is positioned in the fan housing, is kept at the optimum temperature, which results in the viscosity of the lubricating oil remaining reasonably constant under extremes of climatic conditions and with the engine under permanent load.

Transmission. The clutch is of the dry, single-disc type. The four-speed gearbox is fitted with synchromesh on second, third and fourth gears. The gears are helically cut for silent operation.

The rear axle is of the floating half-axle type. The rear wheels are independently sprung through adjustable, circular-section torsion bars. Rebound at front and rear is checked by four hydraulic, double-acting, telescopic shock absorbers.

Chassis. The chassis of the 1200 is of pressed steel. The electrically-welded tubular backbone is forked at the rear to accommodate the transmission and engine unit. The front axle is bolted to the forward end of the chassis and consists of two tubes placed one above the other, containing the laminated torsion bars, at the ends of which are fitted the upper and lower arms of the front-wheel suspension, thus giving independent front-wheel suspension.

Brakes. Lockheed hydraulic brakes are fitted to the de luxe and convertible models, with a separate mechanically-operated handbrake, acting on the rear wheels only. On the standard model the complete braking system is mechanically operated.

The 1200A. The VW 1200A is powered by the 41·5 b.h.p. (gross) engine of the Export or De Luxe 1200 model. The chassis and body of the 1200A and 1300 (*see* page 8) are identical, and the 1200A is also fitted with an improved front axle which has the modified steering gear, a steering damper and stabilizer.

DATA: 1200 AND 1200A BEETLE MODELS

Engine

1. *Cars from August* 1960 *and Transporter from June* 1960 *onwards*

Bore	77 mm (3·031 in.)
Stroke	64 mm (2·520 in.)
Capacity . .	1,192 c.c. (72·74 cu in.)
Compression ratio .	7·0:1
Valve clearance . .	Inlet 0·008 in. (0·2 mm), exhaust 0·0012 in. (0·3 mm) (to be adjusted when engine is cold)
Brake horsepower (gross) .	41·5 at 3,900 r.p.m.

2. *Transporter from May* 1959 *to June* 1960, as in (1) except:

Compression ratio . .	6·6:1
Valve clearance . .	Inlet 0·004 in. (0·1 mm), exhaust 0·008 in. (0·2 mm)
Brake horsepower (gross) .	36 at 3,700 r.p.m.

3. *All models from August* 1954 *to May* 1959 *(Transporter) and August* 1960
   (Cars) as in (2), except:
   Valve clearance . . Inlet and exhaust 0·004 in. (0·1 mm)

4. *All models from January* 1954 *to August* 1954 as in (3), except:
   Compression ratio . . 6·1:1
   Brake horsepower (gross) . 30 at 3,400 r.p.m.

5. *All models up to January* 1954:
   Bore . . . . 75 mm (2·953 in.)
   Stroke . . . . 64 mm (2·520 in.)
   Capacity . . . 1,131 c.c. (69·014 cu in.)
   Compression ratio . . 5·8:1
   Valve clearance . . Inlet and exhaust 0·006 in. (0·15 mm)
   Brake horsepower (gross) . 25 at 3,300 r.p.m.

Ignition Timing
   All models from August 1969 onwards . . $7\frac{1}{2}°$ b.t.d.c.
   Cars from August 1960, Transporter June 1960
   to August 1969 . . . . . 10° b.t.d.c.
   All models from January 1954 to June 1960
   (Transporter) and August 1960 (Cars) . . $7\frac{1}{2}°$ b.t.d.c.
   All models up to January 1954 . . . 5° b.t.d.c.

Contact-breaker Point Gap (all models) . . 0·016 in. (0·4 mm)

Sparking Plugs (all models) . . . . Champion L88 or L87Y
   Sparking plug gap (all models) . . . 0·028 in. (0·7 mm)

Firing Order (all models) 1, 4, 3, 2

Refill Capacities (all models)

Rear Axle and Transmission:			
Up to May 1959 (Transporter) and August 1960 (Cars).	$3\frac{1}{2}$ Imp Pints	$4\frac{1}{4}$ U.S. Pints	2 litres
Later models . .	$4\frac{1}{2}$ Imp Pints	$5\frac{1}{4}$ U.S. Pints	$2\frac{1}{2}$ litres
Reduction gear casings (Transporter) . .	$\frac{1}{2}$ Imp Pint	$\frac{1}{2}$ U.S. Pint	$\frac{1}{4}$ litre
Fuel tank . . .	$8\frac{3}{4}$ Imp Gal	10 U.S. Gal	40 litres
Sump	$4\frac{1}{2}$ Imp Pints	$5\frac{1}{4}$ U.S. Pints	$2\frac{1}{2}$ litres
Brake reservoir . .	$\frac{1}{2}$ Imp Pint	$\frac{1}{2}$ U.S. Pint	$\frac{1}{4}$ litre
Oil-bath air cleaner .	$\frac{1}{2}$ Imp Pint	$\frac{1}{2}$ U.S. Pint	$\frac{1}{4}$ litre

Dimensions and Weights (Approx.

Cars (except Karmann-Ghia)

Length	13 ft 4 in. (4·064 m)
Width	5 ft 6 in. (1·537 m)
Height	4 ft 11 in. (1·499 m)
Ground clearance . . .	6 in. (152 mm)
Unladen weight, ready for use	
Up to August 1964, Saloon .	14 cwt 63 lb (739·8 kg)
Convertible . .	14 cwt 96 lb (754·8 kg)
From August 1964, Saloon .	14 cwt 107 lb (759·8 kg)
Convertible . .	15 cwt 84 lb (800 kg)

Karmann-Ghia

Length	13 ft 7 in. (3·966 m)
Width	5 ft 4 in. (1·526 m)
Height	4 ft 4 in. (1·221 m)
Ground clearance . . .	6 in. (152 mm)
Unladen weight, ready for use .	15 cwt 102 lb (808 kg)

Transporter

Length	14 ft 1 in. (4·293 m)
Width	5 ft 9 in. (1·753 m)
with enlarged platform . .	6 ft 7 in. (2·007 m)
with enlarged wooden platform .	6 ft 6 in. (1·981 m)
Height	6 ft 4 in.–6 ft 5 in. (1·930–1·956 m)
Pick-up, double cab with tarpaulin .	7 ft 3 in. (2·210 m)
High-roofed Delivery Van .	7 ft (2·134 m)
Ground clearance . . .	9½ in. (241 mm)
Unladen weight, ready for use	
Delivery van	20 cwt 42 lb (1035 kg)
Pick-up without tarpaulin . .	20 cwt 108 lb (1065 kg)
Pick-up with tarpaulin . .	21 cwt 73 lb (1050 kg)
Double cab without tarpaulin .	22 cwt 105 lb (1165 kg)
with enlarged platform . .	21 cwt 106 lb (1067 kg)
with enlarged wooden platform .	22 cwt 42 lb (1137 kg)
Kombi	22 cwt 5 lb (1120 kg)
Microbus	22 cwt 16 lb (1125 kg)
Ambulance	24 cwt 13 lb (1225 kg)
Fire truck	22 cwt 82 lb (1156 kg)

Tyres (*see* pages 109 and 115)

Cars

Size (cross-ply) . .	5·60 × 15	
Pressure . . .	Front: 16 lb/sq in.	Rear: 20 lb/sq in.
	1·1 kg/sq cm	1·4 kg/sq cm
Fully laden . . .	Front: 17 lb/sq in.	Rear: 23 lb/sq in.
	1·2 kg/sq cm	1·6 kg/sq cm
Size (radial-ply) . .	155 SR 15 (with tubes)	
Pressure . . .	Front: 18 lb/sq in.	Rear: 27 lb/sq in.
	1·3 kg/sq cm	1·9 kg/sq cm

Transporter

Model	¾ Ton up to Chassis No. 1 222 025		1 Ton		¾ Ton from Chassis No. 1 222 026	
Tyre size . .	6·40–15 with tube		7·00–14 tubeless			
	front	rear	front	rear	front	rear
Pressures lb/sq in. (kg/sq cm)						
up to ¾ payload .	28 (1·9)	30 (2·1)	28 (1·9)	33 (2·3)	28 (1·9)	33 (2·3)
fully loaded .	28 (1·9)	33 (2·3)	28 (1·9)	40 (2·8)	28 (1·9)	30 (2·1)
Ambulance .	26 (1·8)	26 (1·8)	—	—	26 (1·8)	26 (1·8)

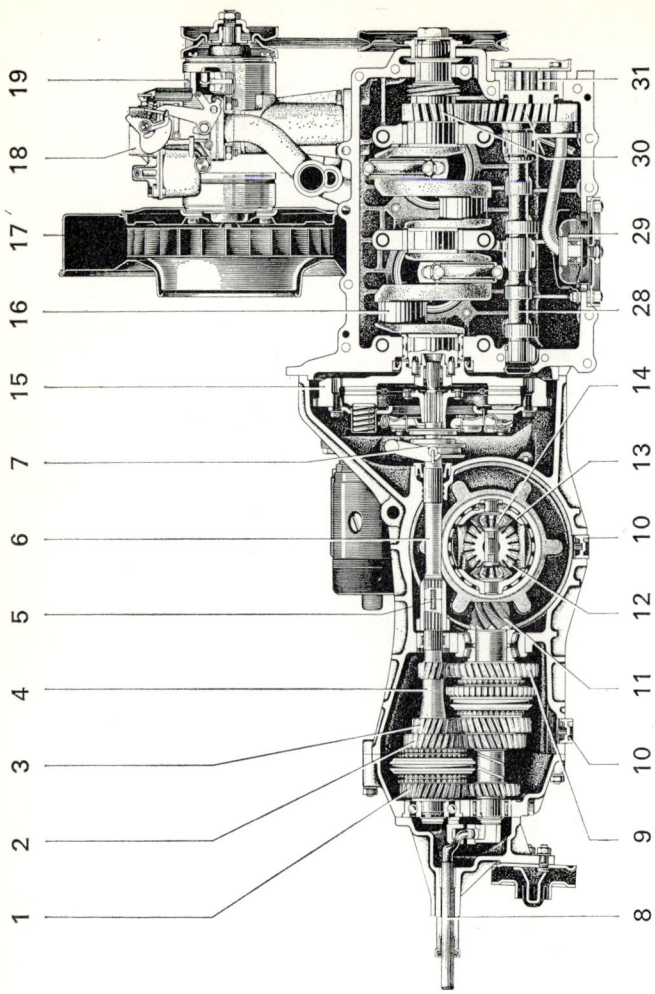

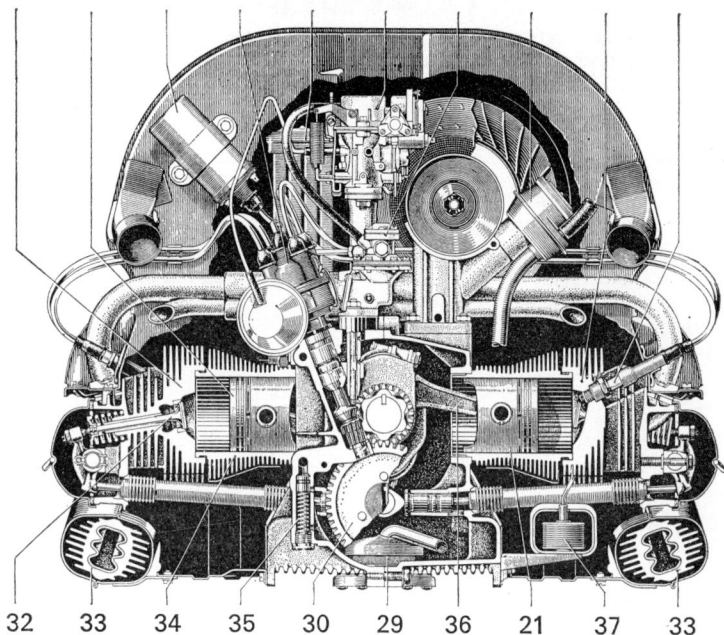

FIG. 1 ENGINE AND TRANSMISSION OF THE 1200, 1300 AND 1500

1. 4th gear
2. 3rd gear
3. 2nd gear
4. Drive shaft, front
5. Reverse gear
6. Drive shaft, rear
7. Clutch release bearing
8. Transmission shift lever
9. 1st gear
10. Oil drain plugs
11. Drive pinion
12. Differential side gear
13. Differential housing
14. Differential pinion
15. Flywheel
16. Crankshaft
17. Fan
18. Carburettor
19. Generator
20. Cylinder head
21. Piston
22. Ignition coil
23. Distributor
24. Oil cooler
25. Fuel pump
26. Oil filler and breather
27. Sparking plug
28. Camshaft
29. Oil strainer
30. Camshaft drive gears
31. Oil pump
32. Valve
33. Heat exchanger
34. Cylinder
35. Oil pressure relief valve
36. Connecting rod
37. Thermostat

THE VW 1300 BEETLE MODELS

The VW 1300 represented a further step in the development of the now classic "Beetle." The familiar 1200 shape was continued but some 23 improvements and changes were made.

The "Super-beetle" is powered by a 50 b.h.p. (gross) engine, giving better acceleration and a higher cruising speed. This 1,285 c.c. engine is of basically similar design to the 41·5 b.h.p. (gross) engine of the 1200 with its well-proven qualities of long service life, economical operation and reliability.

The 1300 is fitted with an improved design of front axle, the steering knuckles and torsion arms being connected by maintenance-free ball joints. The grease nipples that remain require lubrication only at 6,000-mile intervals. Improvements to the transmission increase service life and the unsprung weight is reduced by slotted wheel discs which also improve brake cooling.

DATA: 1300 MODELS

Engine

Bore	77 mm (3·031 in.)
Stroke	69 mm (2·72 in.)
Capacity . . .	1,285 c.c. (78·41 cu in.)
Compression ratio . .	7·3–1
Valve clearance . .	Inlet and exhaust 0·004 in. (0·1 mm) (engine cold)
Brake horsepower . .	50 at 4,600 r.p.m.

Ignition Timing . . . . 7·5° b.t.d.c.

Contact-breaker Point Gap . . 0·016 in. (0·4 mm)

Sparking Plugs . . . Champion L88 or L87Y and plugs of similar grade from other manufacturers

Sparking plug gap . . . 0·028 in. (0·7 mm)

Firing Order 1, 4, 3, 2

Refill Capacities (approx.)

	Imp Gal	U.S. Gal	Litres
Fuel tank	$8\frac{3}{4}$	$10\frac{2}{3}$	40

	Imp Pints	U.S. Pints	Litres
Sump	$4\frac{1}{3}$	$5\frac{1}{3}$	2·5
Rear axle and transmission .	$4\frac{1}{3}$	$5\frac{1}{3}$	2·5
Brake reservoir . . .	$\frac{1}{2}$	$\frac{1}{2}$	0·25
Oil-bath air cleaner . . .	$\frac{1}{2}$	$\frac{1}{2}$	0·25

Dimensions and Weights (approx.)

	Saloon and Convertible	Karmann-Ghia Models
Length . . .	13 ft 2½ in. (4·026 m)	13 ft 7 in. (4·140 m)
Width . . .	5 ft 0½ in. (1·537 m)	5 ft 4 in. (1·626 m)
Height . . .	4 ft 11 in. (1·499 m)	4 ft 4½ in. (1·334 m)
Ground clearance .	6 in. (152 mm)	6 in. (152 mm)
Unladen weight . .	15¼–16¼ cwt (775–826 kg)	16⅜ cwt (830 kg)

Tyres (*see* pages 109 and 115)

	Cross-ply	Radial-ply (with tubes)
Size . .	5·60–15	155 SR 15
Pressure .	Front: 16 lb/sq in. (1·1 kg/sq cm)	18 lb/sq in. (1·3 kg/sq cm)
	Rear: 24 lb/sq in. (1·7 kg/sq cm)	27 lb/sq in. (1·9 kg/sq cm)
Fully laden	Front: 17 lb/sq in. (1·2 kg/sq cm)	18 lb/sq in. (1·3 kg/sq cm)
	Rear: 25 lb/sq in. (1·8 kg/sq cm)	27 lb/sq in. (1·9 kg/sq cm)

THE 1500 BEETLE MODELS

In August 1966 a 1500 c.c. model of the Beetle was introduced. This should not be confused with the VW 1500 with conventional body which was replaced by the 1600A. In spite of its name the 1600A has a 1500 c.c. engine.

The Beetle 1500, with its 53 (gross) b.h.p. engine proved more than a match for its competitors, having considerably increased pulling power and a top speed of approximately 78 m.p.h. for the saloon and 82 m.p.h. for the more aerodynamic Karmann-Ghia model.

Various detail modifications were made, including a new oil-bath air cleaner and provision for drawing pre-heated air into the carburettor to prevent carburettor-icing in cold, damp weather. Disc brakes, similar to those used on the 1600TL and A were fitted to the front wheels and the rear suspension was modified to reduce the oversteer which is associated with these models. Another modification which was welcomed by enthusiastic drivers was a higher third-gear ratio, which improved acceleration in the 55–65 m.p.h. speed range.

A semi-automatic transmission, consisting of a torque converter, coupled to a normal three-speed synchromesh gearbox through a single-plate dry clutch, was offered as an optional alternative to the standard transmission. The clutch is operated hydraulically and is controlled by a valve which is actuated by a solenoid switch whenever the gear lever knob is moved.

The clutch is used only to disconnect the engine from the transmission so that a gear can be selected. When it is re-engaged the drive is taken up smoothly and progressively by the torque converter. Care must be taken, however, not to move the gear lever accidentally as this will disengage the clutch and removal of the load from the engine may cause it to race, putting a considerable strain on the transmission when the plate clutch re-engages as soon as the gear lever is released.

The semi-automatic gearbox has three forward and one reverse driving ranges. They have been designed in such a way that you will very quickly know which driving range is the correct one to use and to give the best advantages under the traffic conditions at the time.

Driving range 1 or the load range is seldom needed. It is necessary for moving off on steep slopes with a full load or when towing a trailer. This range is also recommended for particularly slow driving over difficult ground. Speeds from 0 to 35 m.p.h. can be obtained.

Driving range 2—the moving off and acceleration range—covers from 0 to 55 m.p.h. This range is also recommended for use in heavy city traffic, slow-moving lines of vehicles and whenever maximum acceleration is required for overtaking.

Driving range 3 is the normal range which should be used on the open road. Even in town traffic which is moving freely, although the speeds are relatively low, you can still drive in comfort in this range.

The reverse driving range should, as usual, be engaged only when the vehicle is stationary. The selector lever must be depressed to engage this range.

The neutral position of the selector lever lies between driving ranges 2 and 3, which are the ones you will use most. To select driving range 1 or R the selector lever has first to be pressed to the left.

Starting the engine is possible only when the selector lever is in neutral.

Driving. Before selecting a driving range, depress the footbrake slightly or apply the handbrake. If you like quiet, smooth driving—which saves petrol—select driving range 3 soon after moving off, at about 18–25 m.p.h.

In this range you can drive at practically all speeds right down to a crawl. The torque converter in the transmission changes the power from the engine in an infinitely variable ratio according to the conditions prevailing.

To take full advantage of the acceleration you can stay in driving range 2 right up to 55 m.p.h. and then select driving range 3. This method of driving does, of course, use a little more fuel.

Driving downhill. To make full use of the braking power of the engine, select a lower driving range.

Parking. The vehicle is not prevented from rolling back by engaging a driving range. Always use the handbrake when parking.

When manoeuvring in confined spaces it is advisable to use the driving ranges, Reverse and 1. Select reverse only when the vehicle is stationary and the engine is idling.

Warning light in the speedometer. If you have to drive for a prolonged period under heavy-load conditions, such as when pulling a trailer in a long line of traffic on a hill, the red warning lamp in the speedometer may light up. This means that the temperature of the fluid in the converter has risen considerably. To speed up the cooling rate, first change from driving range 3 to 2. The light will then go out. If it lights up again, you will have to select range 1. The temperature of the converter fluid will then fall to a safe figure.

Towing a trailer. It is better to use driving range 1 for moving off with this extra load and to select a lower range in ample time on gradients.

Tow-starting. The car should be towed at a speed of about 15 m.p.h. with driving range 1 selected. Push-starting is not possible because the transmission of power through the torque converter is not sufficient at slow speeds.

An added benefit of the semi-automatic transmission is that the rear suspension is modified to a diagonal trailing link design with double-jointed axle driving shafts. This virtually eliminates all the previous oversteer tendencies of this model.

Data: 1500 Beetle Model

Except for the engine and the optional semi-automatic transmission, the 1500 Beetle is identical, as far as servicing is concerned, to the 1300 model. The details given on pages 8 and 9 therefore apply, except for the following differences—

Engine

Bore	.	.	.	83 mm (3·27 in.)
Capacity	.	.	.	1,493 c.c. (91·1 cu in.)
Compression ratio	.		.	7·5:1
Brake horsepower	.		.	53 at 4,200 r.p.m.

Capacities

Automatic transmission
  converter system   .   .   approx. 6·3 Imp pints (7·6 U.S. pints, 3·6 litres). Check with VW dealer

Automatic transmission
  and differential   .   ,   5·3 Imp pints (6·3 U.S. pints, 3 litres) hypoid oil (topping up and changes)

MAINTENANCE: 1500 BEETLE MODELS

The maintenance of these cars is the same as for the 1200 and 1300 models described in later chapters. When a semi-automatic transmission is fitted, however, the following additional checks should be made at the 6,000-mile service by a VW dealer—

Check drive shaft sleeves for leaks and damage
Check clutch servo piston-rod clearance
Clean control valve filter
Check gear lever switch contacts, clean or exchange them if necessary
  and adjust the gap

Remove rear brake drums and axle shafts, clean and inspect rear-wheel bearings and fill with new grease.

FIG. 2. THE VW 1500 SALOON

THE VW 1500, 1500A AND 1500S MODELS

The 1500 model with conventional bodywork, first shown publicly at the Frankfort Motor Show in 1961, is outwardly a very different car from the traditional "Beetle," with the appearance of a conventional saloon, but most of the well-tried Volkswagen features are retained.

FIG. 3. THE 1500 ESTATE CAR OR VARIANT

The 1500 c.c. chassis has an improved front suspension layout, in which round-section torsion bars are used instead of superimposed laminated torsion springs. The rear suspension is similar to that on the smaller car.

The VW 1500 engine is more compact than the 1200 model, the height from the sump to the top of the unit being approximately 15 in. As on the smaller car, the cylinders are air-cooled by a centrifugal fan, mounted vertically at the rear of the power unit and in this case driven directly by the crankshaft. On the 1500 engine, a single horizontal Solex carburettor is used. The more powerful 1500S power unit has twin downdraught Solex carburettors, raising the power output from 53 b.h.p. to 66 b.h.p.

After the introduction of the VW 1600 models, the 1500 c.c. models were continued as the 1500A and 1500 Variant (available only to special order in the U.K.), with the single-carburettor engine and with many of the modifications of the 1600 models—for example, improved front axle and transmission, disc brakes on the front wheels and slotted wheel discs.

DATA: 1500 MODELS

Engine

Bore	.	.	.	83 mm (3·27 in.)
Stroke	.	.	.	69 mm (2·72 in.)
Capacity .	.	:	.	1,493 c.c. (91·09 cu in.)
Compression ratio	.	.	1500 and Transporter to August 1965: 7·8 : 1
				Transporter from August 1965: 7·5 : 1
				1500S and Karmann-Ghia: 8·5 : 1

Valve clearance . . Inlet and exhaust: 1500, 0·008 in. (0·2 mm) 1500S, Karmann-Ghia and Transporter to August 1965, 0·012 in. (0·3 mm). Transporter from August 1965, 0·004 in. (0·1 mm)

Brake horsepower . . 1500, 53 at 4,000 r.p.m.
(gross) 1500S and Karmann-Ghia, 66 at 4,800 r.p.m . Transporter up to August 1965, 51 at 3,900 r.p.m.
Transporter from August 1965, 53 at 4,200 r.p.m.

Ignition Timing . . 10° b.t.d.c. from August 1966; previously 7·5° b.t.d.c.

Contact-breaker Point Gap . 0·016 in. (0·4 mm)

Sparking Plugs . . . Champion L 87Y or L 88

Sparking plug gap . . 0·028 in. (0·7 mm)

Firing Order . . . 1, 4, 3, 2

Refill Capacities (approx.)

	Imp Gal	U.S. Gal	Litres
Fuel tank	$8\frac{3}{4}$	10	40
	Imp Pints	**U.S. Pints**	**Litres**
Sump	$4\frac{1}{2}$	$5\frac{1}{3}$	2·5
Brake fluid reservoir . . .	$\frac{1}{2}$	$\frac{1}{2}$	0·25
Oil-bath air cleaner . . .	$\frac{1}{2}$	$\frac{1}{2}$	0·25
Rear axle and transmission .	$4\frac{1}{2}$	$5\frac{1}{3}$	2·5
Reduction gear case (Transporter)	$\frac{1}{2}$	$\frac{1}{2}$	0·25

Dimensions (approx.)

	Length	Width	Height	Ground Clearance
Saloon and Estate Car Variant .	13 ft $10\frac{1}{4}$ in. (4·223 m)	5 ft $3\frac{1}{4}$ in. (1·607 m)	4 ft 10 in. (1·473 m)	6 in. (152 mm)
Karmann-Ghia .	14 ft $0\frac{1}{2}$ in. (4·280 m)	5 ft $3\frac{3}{4}$ in. (1·619 m)	4 ft $4\frac{1}{2}$ in. (1·334 m)	$5\frac{1}{2}$ in. (140 mm)

Unladen Weight (approx.)

1500 Saloon	17 cwt 36 lb (880 kg)
Estate Car Variant 827 lb (375 kg) .	19 cwt 43 lb (985 kg)
Estate Car Variant 1,013 lb (459 kg).	19 cwt 65 lb (995 kg)
1500S Saloon	17 cwt 102 lb (910 kg)
Estate Car Variant . .	20 cwt 19 lb (1025 kg)
Karmann-Ghia . . .	17 cwt 80 lb (900 kg)
Transporter 1500 . . .	See Transporter 1200 figures but note:

1. Models from August 1965 have $\frac{1}{2}$ in. (13 mm) less ground clearance and $\frac{1}{2}$ in. (13 mm) less height.

2. High-roofed Delivery Van has overall height of 7 ft $5\frac{3}{4}$ in. (2·285 m).

Tyres (*see* pages 109 and 115)

Model (Cars fitted with 4½ J wheels)	Cross-ply	Radial-ply (with tubes)
1500 Saloon and Estate Car Variant 827 lb (375 kg)	6·00–15	165 SR 15
Estate Car Variant 1,013 lb (459 kg) .	6·00–15 6 PR	165 SR 15
1500S Saloon and Estate Car Variant 827 lb (375 kg)	6·00–15 L	165 SR 15
Estate Car Variant 1,024 lb (464 kg) .	6·00–15 L 6 PR	165 SR 15
Karmann-Ghia	6·00S–15 L	165 SR 15

Pressures

		Cross-ply	Radial-ply (with tubes)
Saloon and Karmann-Ghia,	Front	16 lb/sq in. (1·1 kg/sq cm)	21 lb/sq in. (1·5 kg/sq cm)
	Rear	24 lb/sq in. (1·7 kg/sq cm)	27 lb/sq in. (1·9 kg/sq cm)
Variants,	Front	17 lb/sq in. (1·2 kg/sq cm)	20 lb/sq in. (1·4 kg/sq cm)
	Rear	24 lb/sq in. (1·7 kg/sq cm)	31 lb/sq in. (2·2 kg/sq cm)

Variant 1,024 lb: When fully loaded, increase rear tyre pressures by 18 lb/sq in., 1·3 kg/sq cm (cross-ply) and 15 lb/sq in., 1·1 kg/sq cm (radial-ply).

Other Variants: When fully loaded, increase rear tyre pressures by 12 lb/sq in., 0·8 kg/sq cm (cross-ply) and 10 lb/sq in., 0·7 kg/sq cm (radial-ply).

Transporters: See figures for 1200 models.

THE 1600 MODELS

The VW 1600 TL, introduced in August 1965, is a five-seater passenger saloon, powered by a rear-mounted, twin-carburettor 1584 c.c. engine which is similar in general design to the 1500S model. The power output is 65 b.h.p. (gross), and the maximum torque 87 ft lb, covering a wide revolution range and giving a top speed of over 85 m.p.h. The compression ratio is 7·7:1 with a fuel octane requirement of 90. Disc brakes are fitted on the front wheels and drum brakes on the rear.

In August 1967, major changes to the 1600 range were announced. A 1500 c.c. engine was introduced as an alternative to the 1600 c.c. models, details of which are given in the data table on page 18. A fully automatic

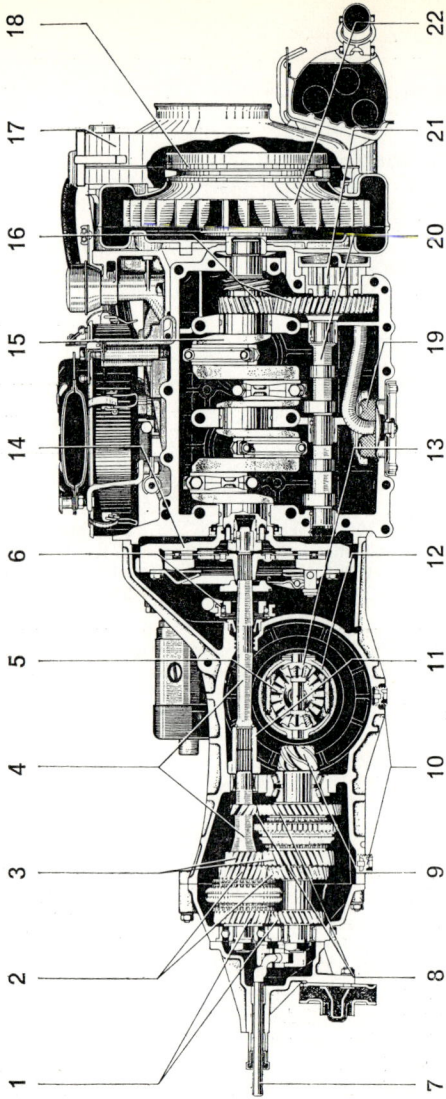

FIG. 4. (*Key on facing page*)

transmission was also available as an alternative to the standard transmission on the 1600L models. This is a three-speed planetary gearbox driven through a three-element torque converter. There are three "drive" positions for the selector, plus neutral, reverse and parking. In "3," gear changes take place automatically, with full-throttle kick-down to a lower ratio if required. With the lever at "1" or "2", the appropriate ratio is immediately engaged and held.

When automatic transmission is fitted, the rear suspension is modified to a trailing-arm design with two universal joints in each drive shaft. This gives greatly improved roadholding and virtually eliminates any oversteer tendency.

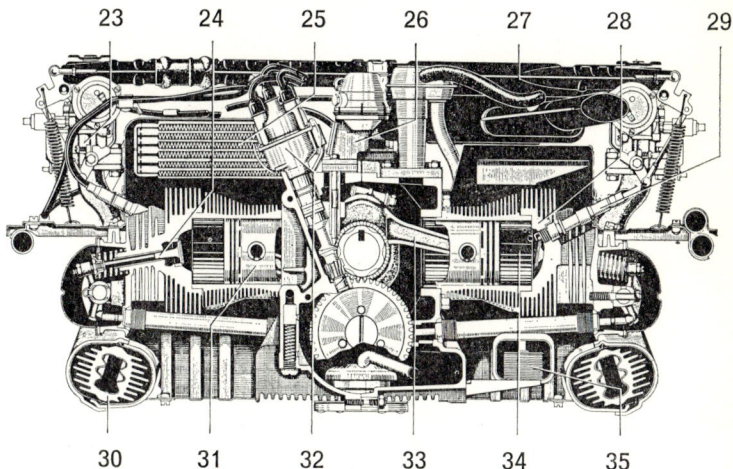

Fig. 4. Engine and Transmission of the 1600L and TL

1. 4th gear train	19. Oil strainer
2. 3rd gear train	20. Camshaft
3. 2nd gear train	21. Oil pump
4. Main drive shaft	22. Fan
5. Differential pinion	23. Carburettor
6. Clutch release bearing	24. Valve
7. Transmission shift lever	25. Oil cooler
8. 1st gear train	26. Fuel pump
9. Drive pinion	27. Oil-bath air cleaner
10. Oil drain plugs	28. Cylinder head
11. Reverse gear	29. Sparking plug
12. Differential housing	30. Heat exchanger
13. Differential pinion	31. Piston
14. Flywheel	32. Ignition distributor
15. Crankshaft	33. Connecting rod
16. Camshaft drive gears	34. Cylinder
17. Fan housing	35. Thermostat
18. Crankshaft pulley	

Fig. 5. The 1600 TL "Fastback" Saloon

DATA: 1600L, TL, T, A AND TA MODELS

Engine	1600L, TL, T, TA and 1600A Variant	1600A Saloon
Bore . . .	85·5 mm (3·36 in.)	83 mm (3·27 in.)
Stroke . . .	69 mm (2·72 in.)	69 mm (2·72 in.)
Capacity . . .	1,584 c.c. (96·6 cu in.)	1,493 c.c. (91·1 cu in.)
Compression ratio .	7·7:1	7·5:1
Valve clearance (engine cold) . .	0·004 in. (0·1 mm)	0·004 in. (0·1 mm)
Brake horsepower .	65 at 4,600 r.p.m.	54 at 4,200 r.p.m.
Sparking Plugs . .	Champion L88 or L87Y	Champion L88 or L87Y
	or plugs of similar grades	
Sparking plug gap .	0·028 in. (0·7 mm)	0·028 in. (0·7 mm)
Contact-breaker Gap .	0·016 in. (0·4 mm)	0·016 in. (0·4 mm)
Ignition Timing,		
Manual . . .	7.5° b.t.d.c.	7.5° b.t.d.c.
Automatic . .	0° b.t.d.c.	—
Firing Order . . .	1, 4, 3, 2	1, 4, 3, 2

Refill Capacities (approx.)

	Imp Gal	U.S. Gal	Litres
Fuel tank	$8\frac{3}{4}$	$10\frac{2}{3}$	40

	Imp Pints	U.S. Pints	Litres
Engine	$4\frac{1}{3}$	$5\frac{1}{3}$	2·5
Rear axle and transmission .	$4\frac{1}{3}$	$5\frac{1}{3}$	2·5
Brakes	$\frac{1}{2}$	$\frac{1}{2}$	0·25
Oil-bath air cleaner . . .	$\frac{2}{3}$	$\frac{3}{4}$	0·38

Dimensions and Weights (approx.)

	Up to August 1969		From August 1969	
	Saloon	Estate Car Variant	Saloon	Estate Car Variant
Length . .	13 ft $10\frac{1}{4}$ in. (4·223 m)		14 ft 3 in. (4·343 m)	
Width . .	5 ft $3\frac{1}{4}$ in. (1·607 m)		5 ft 5 in. (1·651 m)	5 ft 4 in. (1·626 m)
Height . .	4 ft 10 in. (1·473 m)		4 ft 10 in. (1·473 m)	
Ground clearance.	6 in. (152 mm)		6 in. (152 mm)	
Unladen weight .	19 cwt 108 lb (1014 kg)	20 cwt 19 lb (1025 kg)	18 cwt 100 lb (960 kg)	19 cwt 62 lb (993 kg)

Tyres (*see* pages 109 and 115)

Size (cross-ply)

Saloon and Estate car variant (826 lb,
375 kg) .   .   .   .   .   .   6·00 × 15L
Estate car Variant (1,025 lb, 465 kg)   .   6·00 × 15L6 PR

Pressures

Saloon.   .   Front, 16 lb/sq in. (1·1 kg/sq cm)
               Rear, 24 lb/sq in. (1·7 kg/sq cm)
Fully laden .   Front, 18 lb/sq in. (1·3 kg/sq cm)
               Rear, 27 lb/sq in. (1·8 kg/sq cm)

Estate car

Variant   .   Front, 17 lb/sq in. (1·2 kg/sq cm)
               Rear, 26 lb/sq in. (1·8 kg/sq cm)
Fully laden .   Front, 17 lb/sq in. (1·2 kg/sq cm)
               Rear: 826 lb Variant, 37 lb/sq in. (2·6 kg/sq cm)
               Rear: 1,025 lb Variant, 45 lb/sq in. (3·2 kg/sq cm)

Size (radial-ply)

All models	.	.	.	. 165 SR 15 (with tubes)
Pressures	.	.	.	. Front, 18 lb/sq in. (1·3 kg/sq cm)
				Rear, 27 lb/sq in. (1·9 kg/sq cm)
Fully laden, Variant 826 lb.	.		.	Rear, 35 lb/sq in. (2·5 kg/sq cm)
1,025 lb.	.	.	.	. Rear, 40 lb/sq in. (2·8 kg/sq cm)

VOLKSWAGEN 1968 AND LATER MODEL COMMERCIALS

The 1968-model Commercial vehicle or Transporter, introduced in August 1967, is available for the usual wide range of applicatons, including versions of the van, pick-up truck, Kombi, Clipper (mini-bus) and also a number of motor-caravan conversions.

The commercial vehicle has a 1·6 litre, rear-mounted engine which develops 57 b.h.p. at 4,400 r.p.m. The loading or passenger compartment has a sliding door and individual front seats give direct access from the driving compartment to the interior of the vehicle.

DATA: VOLKSWAGEN 1968-MODEL COMMERCIAL

Specification: Engine as for 1600L and TL models except for the differences listed below, but note that this is a vertical-fan engine of the type illustrated in Fig. 1.

Brake horsepower	.	.	57 at 4,400 r.p.m.
Ignition timing	.	.	t.d.c.

FIG. 6. THE 1968-MODEL COMMERCIAL IN CLIPPER
(MINI-BUS FORM)

Refill Capacities (approx.)

	Imp Gal	U.S. Gal	Litres
Fuel tank	13	16	60
	Imp Pints	U.S. Pints	Litres
Engine	$4\frac{1}{3}$	$5\frac{1}{3}$	2·5
Gearbox and differential . .	6	$7\frac{1}{2}$	3·5
Brakes	$\frac{1}{2}$	$\frac{2}{3}$	0·3
Oil-bath air cleaner . . .	$\frac{3}{4}$	1	0·45

Tyres (*see* pages 109 and 115)
Size, Clipper L .   .   .   185R 14 with tubes
      Clipper   .   .   .   700–14 6PR tubeless
      All other models .   .   700–14 8PR tubeless

Pressures
Front, all models   .   .   .   .   28 lb/sq in. (2 kg/sq cm)
Rear, Clipper L   .   .   .   .   28 lb/sq in. (2 kg/sq cm)
     All other models   .   .   .   35 lb/sq in. (2·5 kg/sq cm)
Rear, full load, Clipper L .   .   .   35 lb/sq in. (2·5 kg/sq cm)
        All other models   .   41 lb/sq in. (2·9 kg/sq cm)

FIG. 7. THE VOLKSWAGEN DELIVERY VAN (FOREGROUND)
this has a single sliding door at the side. Sliding doors on both sides can be supplied at an
additional cost. The pick-up truck is shown in the background.

Dimensions and Weights (approx.)

	Length	Width	Height Unladen	Ground Clearance	Weight Unladen
Clipper L	14 ft 7 in. (4·445 m)	5 ft 11½ in. (1·815 m)	6 ft 4½ in. (1·943 m)	7¼ in. (185 mm)	24 cwt 89 lb (1,260 kg)
Clipper	14 ft 4 in. (4·420 m)	5 ft 9½ in. (1·765 m)	6 ft 4½ in. (1·943 m)	7¼ in. (185 mm)	24 cwt 34 lb (1,235 kg)
Kombi	14 ft 4 in. (4·420 m)	5 ft 9½ in. (1·765 m)	6 ft 4¾ in. (1·950 m)	7¼ in. (185 mm)	24 cwt 100 lb (1,265 kg)
Delivery van	14 ft 4 in. (4·420 m)	5 ft 9½ in. (1·765 m)	6 ft 5 in. (1·955 m)	7¼ in. (185 mm)	23 cwt 14 lb (1,175 kg)
High-roofed delivery van	14 ft 4 in. (4·420 m)	5 ft 9½ in. (1·765 m)	7 ft 6¼ in. (2·290 m)	7¼ in. (185 mm)	24 cwt 67 lb (1,250 kg)
Pick-up, with cover	14 ft 4 in. (4·420 m)	5 ft 9½ in. (1·765 m)	7 ft 4½ in. (2·245 m)	7¼ in. (185 mm)	23 cwt 90 lb (1,210 kg)
without cover	14 ft 4 in. (4·420 m)	5 ft 9½ in. (1·765 m)	6 ft 5 in. (1·955 m)	7¼ in. (185 mm)	23 cwt 14 lb (1,175 kg)

411, 411L, 411E AND 411LE MODELS

The VW 411 model, which was introduced in August 1968, broke away from the Volkswagen tradition in a number of respects. For example, this was the first Volkswagen to have an integral body-chassis construction. Earlier models, of course, had—and still have—separate bodies which are bolted to a platform chassis. On the VW 411, the front suspension and steering assembly, and the rear suspension, power unit and transmission are mounted on separate sub-frames which are bolted to the body.

The torsion-bar suspension systems so long associated with Volkswagens

Fig. 8. The VW 411 and 411E Saloon

were replaced by a coil-spring system, a Macpherson-strut layout being used at the front and a semi-trailing link, independent suspension system at the rear. About the only feature which was recognizably Volkswagen, in fact, was the compact engine and transmission unit, although here another design development was a new four-speed gearbox, in which a direct-drive top gear was used for the first time, the drive passing through a hollow output shaft to the final-drive pinion, through a long quill shaft.

The standard VW heating system was improved by the provision of a petrol-burning booster which can be used to augment the heat provided by the engine or which can be operated while the engine is switched off.

It has been said that the 411 got off to a bad start because photographs and details of the car were published prematurely in the European press, to some extent robbing Volkswagen of the initiative in deciding the most

Fig. 9. A Cross-section through the VW 411 and 411E. The unitary-construction body is of completely new design.

opportune moment to announce the new model. Certainly the 411E and 411LE models, which were announced in August 1969, were an improvement on the earlier cars, the most significant development being the adoption of VW–Bosch electronically-controlled fuel injection as standard equipment. This raised the power of the engine from 76 b.h.p. to 85 b.h.p. and the torque (a measure of pulling power) from 92 lb/ft at 2,800 r.p.m. to 97·6 lb/ft at 2,700 r.p.m., significantly improving the performance.

The addition of an anti-roll bar to the rear suspension reduced the tendency of the car to understeer when cornered fast, although sufficient understeer remained to give the driver confidence even when pressing the car hard—a very different state of affairs, of course, from the over-steering tendencies of the early Beetle models.

DATA: 411, 411L, 411E AND 411LE MODELS

Engine

Bore	90 mm (3·54 in.)
Stroke	66 mm (2·6 in.)
Capacity . . .	1,679 c.c. (125 cu in.)

Compression ratio,

411, 411L . . .	7·8:1
411E, 411LE . .	8·2:1
Valve clearance . . .	0·004 in. (0·1 mm), engine cold

Brake horsepower,

411, 411L . . .	76 at 5,000 r.p.m.
411E, 411LE . .	85 at 5,000 r.p.m.

Sparking plugs,

411, 411L . . .	Champion N–88
411E, 411LE . .	Beru 175/14/3 or N–5—or plugs of similar grade
Sparking plug gap . .	0·028 in. (0·7 mm)
Contact-breaker gap . .	0·016 in. (0·4 mm)
Dwell angle . . .	44°–50° (with vacuum pipe disconnected)

Ignition timing,

Static	5° t.d.c.
Stroboscope . .	27° b.t.d.c. at 3,500 r.p.m. (with vacuum pipe disconnected)
Firing order . . .	1, 4, 3, 2

Refill Capacities (approx.

	Imp Gal	U.S. Gal	Litres
Fuel tank (including reserve) . .	11	13¼	50
	Imp Pints	U.S. Pints	Litres
Engine	5¼	6¼	3
Engine, with filter change . . .	6¼	7½	3·5
Gearbox and final drive . . .	5½	6½	3·125
Automatic transmission, converter and transmission	5¼	6¼	3
Automatic transmission, final drive .	1¾	2	1
Oil bath air cleaner	¾	1	0·45
Brakes	—	⅜	0·19

Tyres (*see* pages 109 and 115)

Size
    411, 411L .   145 SR–15
    411E, 411LE 155 SR–15
    Variant   .   165 SR–15

Pressures

	Front	Rear
Saloon,		
normal .	20 lb/sq in. (1·4 kg/sq cm)	26 lb/sq in. (1·8 kg/sq cm)
fully laden.	23 lb/sq in. (1·6 kg/sq cm)	30 lb/sq in. (2·1 kg/sq cm)
Variant,		
normal .	17 lb/sq in. (1·2 kg/sq cm)	28 lb/sq in. (2·0 kg/sq cm)
fully laden.	20 lb/sq in. (1·4 kg/sq cm)	36 lb/sq in. (2·5 kg/sq cm)

For long, high-speed motoring, always use the highest pressures

Dimensions and Weights (approx.)

    Length   .   .   .   .   14 ft 10 in. (4·525 m)
    Width   .   .   .   .   5 ft 4½ in. (1·635 m)
    Height, unladen   .   .   4 ft 10½ in. (1·485 m)
    Ground clearance   .   .   5½ in. (135 mm)
    Unladen weight
        2-door saloon   .   .   20 cwt 8 lb (1020 kg)
        4-door saloon   .   .   20 cwt 52 lb (1040 kg)
        Variant   .   .   .   23 cwt 13 lb (1174 kg)

RECOMMENDED LUBRICANTS

Lubrication Points	Castrol	Esso	Filtrate	Mobil	Regent/Caltex	BP	Shell
Engine* . . .	Castrolite or GTX	Esso Uniflow	"Filtrate" 10W/30	Mobiloil Super	Havoline Special 10W/40	Super V	Shell Super 100
Transmission case . Steering gear .	Castrol Hypoy	Esso Gear Oil GP 90	Hypoid "Filtrate" Gear Oil 90	Mobilube GX 90	Universal Thuban 90	Energol SAE 90 EP	Spirax 90 EP
Front axle . Front wheel bearings Ignition distributor cam Door and hood locks. Brake cables	Castrolease LM	Esso Multi-Purpose Grease H	Super Lithium "Filtrate" Grease	Mobilgrease MP or Mobilgrease Special	Marfak Multi-Purpose 2	Energrease L2	Retinax A

* These recommendations apply also to VW Industrial Engines. Alternative monograde engine oils are: summer, SAE 30; winter, SAE 20; temperatures below −15°C (5°F), SAE 10W; below −25°C (−13°F), SAE 5W. In arctic conditions use SAE 80 oil in the transmission.

2 Routine maintenance

ONLY simple maintenance and servicing is needed to keep your Volkswagen in first-class trim. The work is well within the scope of the practically-minded owner whose resources are limited to the hand tools usually found in the domestic garage and workshop. Apart from the interest and knowledge that one gains in the process, the time spent will pay dividends in better running, lower petrol consumption and replacement costs and will give you a new understanding and affection for the car.

When more ambitious work and major dismantling is necessary, your VW dealer will be ready to advise you and discuss the question of an overhaul or the fitting of reconditioned parts. As this work calls for specialized equipment and some degree of skill and experience, it is outside the scope of this book.

In this chapter the various jobs are dealt with more or less in the order in which they occur in the maintenance charts on pages 29–34. Most of the work should be within the scope of even a novice, but more detailed information will be found in the later chapters, which are devoted to the individual components.

WV Diagnostic System. Although what has been said so far is aimed at the average reader of this book—probably an enthusiastic owner who wishes to carry out as much of the servicing on his car as possible—it would not be realistic to ignore the excellent VW diagnosis and maintenance system, introduced in Britain late in 1969, after having been thoroughly tested in Europe. The system entails a series of more than 50 checks which are carried out at 6,000-mile intervals, electronic engine-testing and tuning equipment, and similar modern aids, being used wherever possible.

A buyer of a new VW is given five free diagnostic vouchers, which take care of the well-being of the car during the first 24,000 miles. These are valid for five years, so that the low-mileage motorist is not penalized. The vouchers take the form of punched cards, which are sent to the appropriate VW depot by the service station, the complete mechanical history of the car being stored in a computer. Only the maintenance jobs that are necessary are done, but the owner receives a written report on the condition of the car, with recommendations concerning any further work that should be carried out.

Owners of pre-1970 VWs can participate in the scheme by paying a

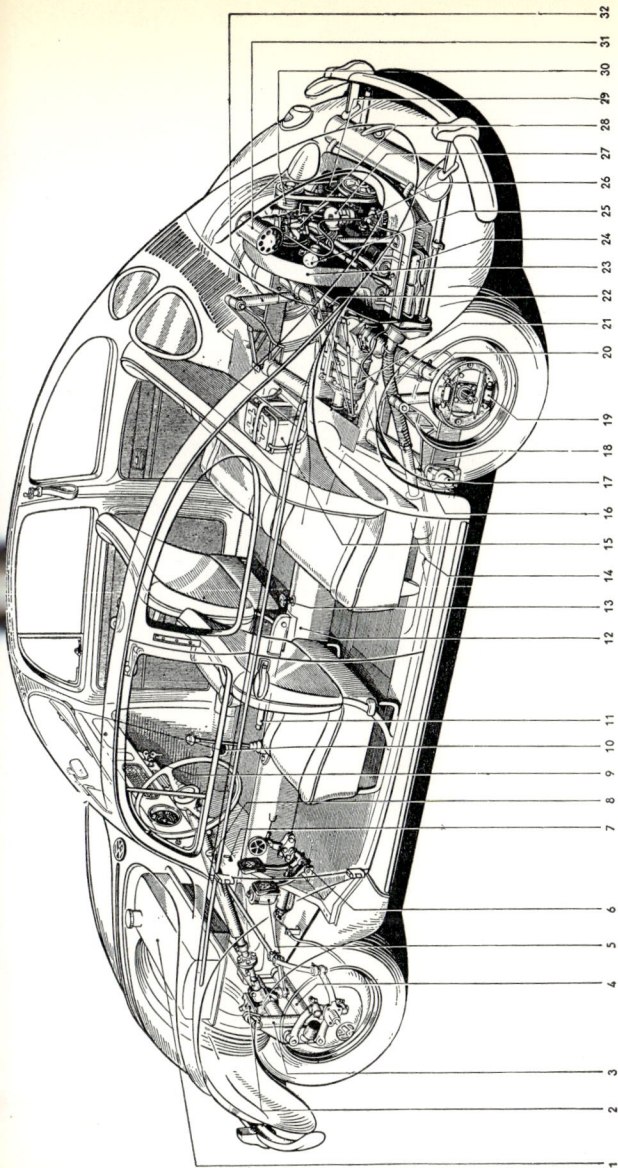

FIG. 10. THE VOLKSWAGEN 1200 SALOON

This model is typical of the 1200 and 1300 range covered by this book, although minor differences will be found in earlier and later cars

1. Fuel tank	8. Bonnet lock control	15. Battery	21. Transmission	27. Distributor
2. Steering gear	9. Choke control	16. Warm air tube	22. Starter	28. Carburettor
3. Shock absorber	10. Warm air vent	17. Torsion bar	23. Fan housing	29. Dipstick
4. Front axle	11. Handbrake lever	18. Spring plate	24. Cylinder head cover	30. Generator
5. Brake master cylinder	12. Frame tunnel	19. Brake wheel cylinder	25. Ignition coil	31. Air cleaner
6. Pedal linkage	13. Heat control	20. Rear axle	26. Fuel pump	32. Shock absorber
7. Fuel tap	14. Warm air vent			

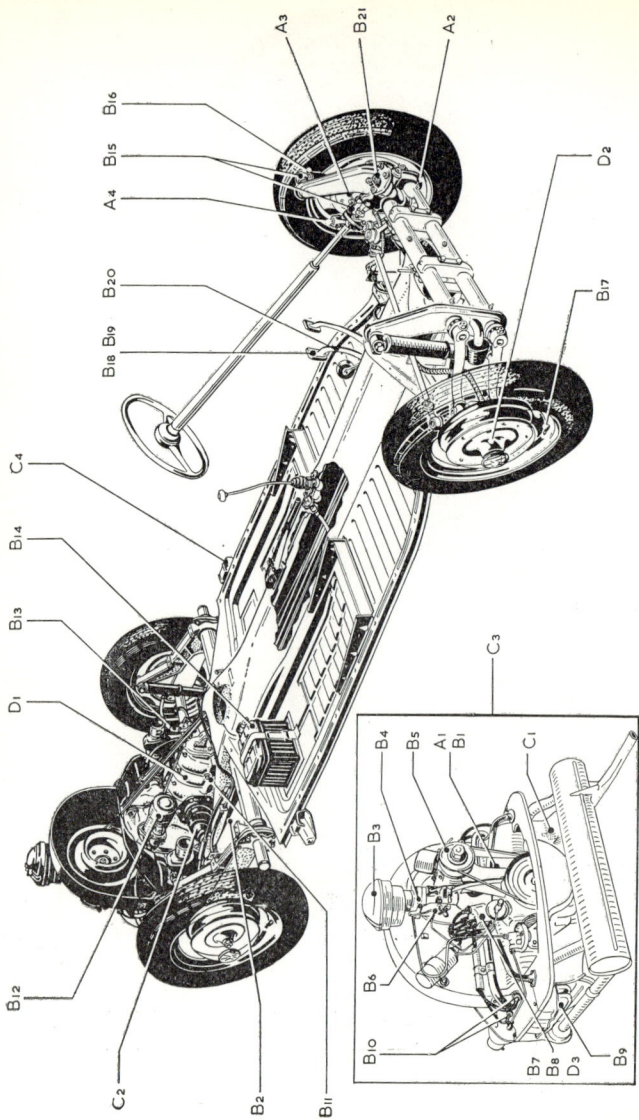

Every 1,500 Miles (approx 2,500 Km)

A1. Check engine oil level. Top-up if necessary
A2, A3. Lubricate front axle (required at 3,000 miles only on 1200 from August 1964, 1200A and 1300)
A4. Lubricate tie-rods (earlier 1200 models only)

Every 3,000 Miles (approx 5,000 Km)

B1. Change engine oil
B2. Clean oil strainer

Every 6,000 Miles (approx 10,000 Km)

B3. Clean air cleaner
B4. Clean carburettor; check adjustment. On later models clean fuel pump filter
B5. Check and adjust fan belt
B6. Lubricate carburettor controls
B7. Two drops of oil on contact-breaker arm fibre block in distributor. Lubricate auto-advance weights
B8. Check contact-breaker points and ignition timing
B9. Check valve clearances
B10. Check sparking plugs and engine compression
B11. Check oil level in transmission and converter (when fitted)
B12. Check generator

Every 6,000 Miles (cont.)

B13. Brake cables—check and lubricate
B14. Examine battery (preferably at 1,500 miles or more often in hot weather)
B15. Check front wheel bearings, front suspension and steering and toe-in
B16. Check tightness and effect of shock absorbers
B17. Check tyre pressures and tighten wheel bolts
B18. Test brakes and check fluid level
B19. Foot pedal group—check and lubricate
B20. Check clutch pedal clearance
B21. Steering gear; check oil level
C1. Check automatic cooling air control
C2. Inspect rear axle and engine for oil leaks
C3. Check tightness of all nuts and bolts on engine; especially exhaust, carburettor, fuel pump and intake manifold
C4. Check all nuts and bolts on chassis, front and rear axles and steering

Every 30,000 Miles (approx 50,000 Km)

D1. Change transmission oil and (on Transporter) reduction gear oil
D2. Front wheel bearings—check for wear and lubricate
D3. Cam bearing in distributor—lubricate

FIG. 11 LUBRICATION AND MAINTENANCE CHART, 1200, 1200A, 1300 AND 1500 BEETLE MODELS

The maintenance of the Transporter is similar. A lubrication chart for any model can be obtained from the
Castrol Chart Library, Castrol House, Marylebone Road, London N.W.1, free of charge.

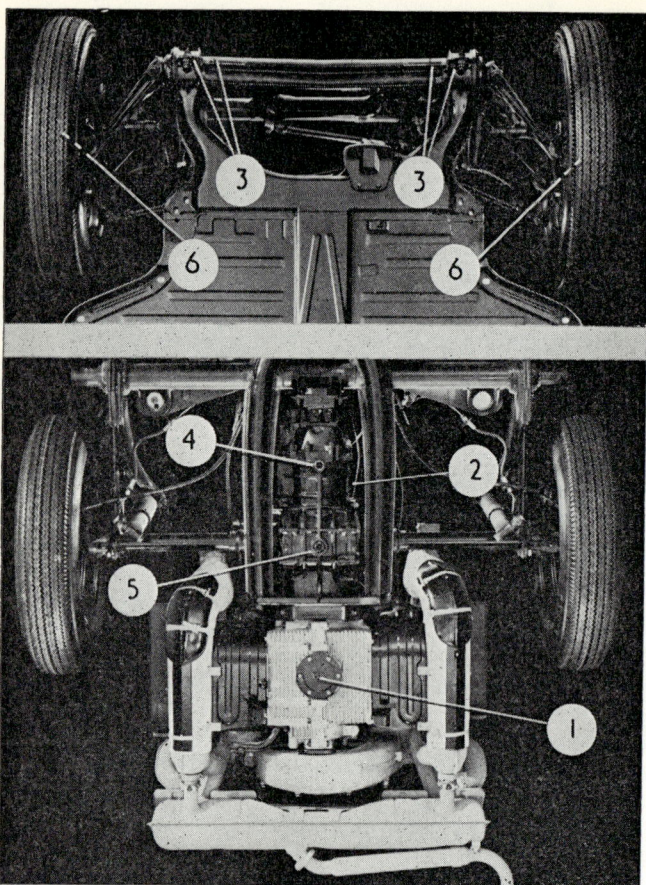

FIG. 12. THE LUBRICATION POINTS SHOWN APPLY SPECIFICALLY TO THE 1500, 1500S AND 1600 MODELS

The 411 models do not require lubrication of the front suspension and steering, but points 1, 2, 4 and 5 are similar in the 411 range.

1. Engine oil filter plate
2. Transmission filler and level plug
3. Front suspension lubrication points

4. Transmission drain plug
5. Final-drive drain plug
6 Front-wheel hubs

LUBRICATION AND MAINTENANCE

1500, 1500S AND 1600 MODELS

The vehicle types referred to in this schedule
are explained on page 1

Every 3,000 Miles (approx 5,000 Km)

Drain engine oil and refill

Remove and clean oil filter and magnetic ring (when fitted)

Lubricate carburettor controls

Lubricate door locks and hinges

Check battery electrolyte level and specific gravity

Clean and grease terminals

Check tyres for wear and damage to casings. Check pressures

Every 6,000 Miles (approx 10,000 Km)

Check oil level in transmission

Vehicles with fully-automatic transmission—Types 3 and 4 only: Check
fluid level in transmission and in separate final-drive casing. Check oil
sump retaining screws for tightness

Vehicles with selector-automatic transmissions—Type 1 only: Clean
control valve air filter. Check selector contacts, clean and adjust if
necessary (best done by a VW dealer). Check fluid level in torque converter oil container. Check tightness of transmission oil-pan retaining
screws

Vehicles with double-joint rear axles—Check constant-velocity joint bolts
for tightness

Lubricate front axle

Check oil level in steering gear—Types 1, 2 and 3

Check front suspension strut ball joints for wear—Type 4 only

Check carburettor air cleaner. Clean out bowl if necessary. Refill with
engine oil. This should be done more frequently if vehicle is driven in
very dusty conditions

Check dynamo belt tension. Adjust if necessary

Check carburettor slow-running adjustment. Every second 6,000-mile
service, clean float chamber and jets

Check fuel pump filter

Check and if necessary replace ignition distributor contact-breaker points.
Check and adjust gap. Lubricate cam and shaft bearing. Check ignition
timing

Clean sparking plugs. Check and re-set gap

Check and if necessary adjust valve clearances

Check rubber valve for crankcase ventilation system

Check exhaust system for damage

Check water drain flaps

Check cooling air bellows

Check clutch adjustment and re-set if necessary

Check tightness of all nuts and bolts. Check for leakage of oil, fuel and brake fluid

Have engine compression tested by VW agent

Check thickness of brake linings

Check hydraulic brake system for leaks and damage, check brake fluid level and adjust hand and foot brakes

Lubricate brake cables—Types 1 and 2

Lubricate pedal cluster—Types 1 and 2

Check operation of brake pressure limiting valve—Type 4 only

Check operation of electrical system. Adjust headlight alignment if necessary

Have VW agent carry out following work on suspension and steering:

    Check and adjust axial play of upper torsion arms, camber and front wheel toe-in. Check and adjust play between steering gear roller and worm

Every 12,000 miles (approx 20,000 Km)

Renew ignition contact-breaker points

Adjust ignition timing

Fit new sparking plugs

Vehicles with fuel-injection system: replace fuel filter—Types 3 and 4 only

Every 30,000 Miles (approx 50,000 Km)

Drain transmission. Clean magnetic drain plugs. Refill with fresh hypoid gear oil

Drain oil from reduction gears on Transporter. Refill with fresh hypoid gear oil

Dismantle front-wheel hubs. Check condition of bearings. Re-lubricate and adjust (preferably to be done by a VW agent)

Vehicles with double-joint rear axles—dismantle and clean rear-wheel bearings; re-pack with grease

Every 2 Years

Pump all fluid out of braking system and refill with new fluid. Check condition of all rubber components. Have pressure-check made on brake limiting valve (Type 4 only) by VW dealer modest fee for the diagnostic checks and will receive the same detailed reports on their cars as in the case of new-car owners. Further information on this scheme will be given by any VW dealer, but it is only fair to point out that routine checks and maintenance jobs can be carried out quite adequately by a practical owner who prefers to do the work himself and it is, of course, the object of this book to provide him with the necessary information to do so.

Lubrication. This is a most important aspect of regular maintenance. Neglect of the simple routine jobs can cause expensive damage or noisy and inefficient operation. Moreover, it should be remembered that the oils and greases recommended in Chapter 1 are carefully refined and blended and special additives may be embodied in them to give certain properties. "Cheap" oils are, therefore, the most expensive in the long run. Good quality oils will more than repay their slight additional cost.

A good engine oil, for example, if it is of the modern additive type, will prevent corrosion of the cylinder walls, inhibit formation of sludge and gum, which can cause sticking of piston rings and valves, and will leave the engine in an exceptionally clean condition as compared with the results obtained from the use of the "straight" oils which were all that were normally available some years ago.

Similarly, the teeth of the gears in the transmission are subject to much higher stresses than the earlier types of gear and these require oils containing special additives to maintain an adequate film of lubricant between the working parts. However good this oil may be initially, it begins to lose some of its properties after a period of service and the transmission must, therefore, be drained and refilled at the mileage specified. Moreover, it is not advisable to mix "extreme pressure" oils, as they are termed, as they do not always take kindly to one another.

The points at which it is necessary to inject grease are shown in Figs. 11 and 12. The hand-operated grease gun used by the owner is an efficient instrument capable of injecting grease at high pressure and overcoming considerable resistance in partially-choked grease passages. In order to ensure that the maximum pressure is developed, however, it is essential that the nipple should be thoroughly cleaned before the gun is applied. Another reason for carefully cleaning the nipple is, of course, to prevent any risk of grit being forced through the nipple into the bearing.

If the nipple is dented or otherwise damaged it is a simple matter to unscrew it and fit a replacement which can be obtained from your VW dealer. In an emergency, however, it is possible to obtain a satisfactory seal even on a damaged nipple if a piece of light fabric is first placed between the nipple and the end of the grease gun.

For oil-can attentions a good-quality light machine oil, or preferably an oil which has anti-rust properties, can be used in an oil can. On parts such as door hings and catches, surplus oil should be wiped off to prevent soiling of driver's or passengers' clothes. A solidified lubricant can be obtained for this purpose which is rather cleaner than ordinary oil. Parts such as the distributor automatic-advance mechanism should not be forgotten; the small weights housed within the distributor body greatly influence the whole behaviour of the engine and the power output, fuel consumption and performance that will be obtained. They should be lubricated as specified under the 6,000-mile heading (see page 38).

Regular Inspections. Every 150–200 miles or before starting on a long run, it is advisable to check the engine oil level with the dip-stick. The level should of course, be topped-up at intervals to bring the oil to the "full" mark. These checks should be made with the car standing on level ground and a short time should always be allowed for the oil to drain back into the crank-case; otherwise a misleading reading may be obtained.

The oil should not be allowed to fall below the danger mark on the dip-stick or serious damage may be caused. If the engine is in good condition, topping-up should be needed only every 200 or 300 miles or at even longer periods when the engine is new; a worn engine, however, will need more frequent checks. Remember, too, that the oil consumption will be quite substantially increased when long, fast runs are undertaken, as compared with the figure that one becomes accustomed to when shorter runs at modest speeds are the order of the day. Tests have shown that the oil does not attain its maximum temperature until the car has been running for approximately one hour.

The tyre pressures should be checked weekly. They should be maintained at the figures given in Chapter 1. If the pressures are unequal or incorrect, the steering, braking, roadholding and tyre life will be adversely affected.

Front Axle and Steering. Reference to the lubrication chart will show the location of the grease nipples which are provided for the lubrication of

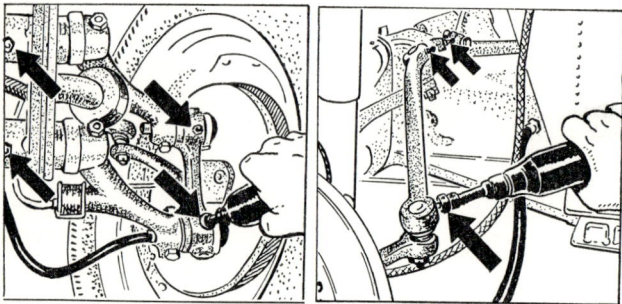

FIG. 13. LUBRICATION POINTS ON THE FRONT
SUSPENSION AND STEERING

the king pins, front axle tubes and tie-rod ends. Three or four strokes of the grease gun are sufficient at each of these points.

On late models, routine maintenance has been considerably reduced by the elimination of lubrication points on the steering connexions, hand-brake cable, clutch release and brake pedal bearings.

It is essential when greasing the suspension and steering to jack up the front of the car until the front wheel is clear of the ground. This will allow grease to cover the thrust faces.

Battery. The wise owner will inspect the level of the electrolyte in the battery at regular intervals, depending on the atmospheric temperature, since the electrolyte will evaporate more quickly in hot weather. It is advisable, however, to check the battery also at intervals of 1,500 miles, adding distilled water to bring the level of the electrolyte to between $\frac{1}{4}$ in. and $\frac{3}{8}$ in. above the separators in the cells. The care of the battery is more fully described in Chapter 6.

Air Cleaner. A dirty air cleaner not only reduces the performance of the engine, but also causes increased fuel consumption. The cleaner should be serviced as described in Chapter 4. When the car is operated under very dusty conditions, more frequent attention will be required.

Changing Engine Oil. The engine oil becomes contaminated with carbon and other products of combustion, including condensed water and fuel, and must, therefore, be drained out at least at 3,000-mile intervals. It is now recommended that the oil filter should be cleaned whenever the oil is drained, whereas in earlier instruction books this job was specified only at 6,000-mile intervals. The method of cleaning the filter is described later, but first one or two notes on changing the oil must be included, mainly for the benefit of the novice.

If the engine is worn, the degree of gas leakage past the piston rings may make it advisable to change the oil more frequently; for example, it is usually recommended that a change at 2,000 miles shows some economy in the long run, since, by maintaining the quality of the oil, the overall consumption is reduced.

Also, more frequent changes are advisable when most of the driving is done in cold weather, particularly when frequent starts are made from cold and when the engine is allowed to idle for long periods. Similarly, in hot, dusty conditions the oil will deteriorate more quickly than in temperate climates.

The oil should be drained when the car has just come in from a run; being hot, the oil will be more fluid and will be holding in suspension the impurities just referred to.

If a modern premium oil is used it should not be necessary to flush out the sump with flushing oil, as was often recommended with older types of car. A sufficiently large drain pan should be provided; an old kitchen washing-up bowl is a useful container for this purpose. On earlier engines the drain plug is at one side of the filter-retaining plate (see Fig. 18); on later engines a plug is fitted at the centre of the plate (Fig. 17). Sufficient time should be allowed for the oil to drain completely before the drain plug is replaced. The sump should then be refilled until the level is up to the "full" mark on the dip-stick.

Distributor. The distributor cap should be removed after springing aside the two securing clips. In most cases the rotor, which is attached to the top of the cam spindle, can be pulled off fairly easily by hand. If it is tight, it should be eased off by rocking it slightly from side to side as a firm upward pull is applied.

When the rotor has been removed a few drops of light oil should be placed on the felt in the cam to allow the oil to lubricate the cam bearing. A few drops of oil should also be applied through the holes in the distributor baseplate to lubricate the governor weight mechanism. Although engine oil may be used for this purpose a good upper cylinder lubricant, such as "Redex" is preferable. This type of oil tends to prevent gumming and also prevents the formation of rust.

A thin film of petroleum jelly should also be applied to the contact-breaker cam faces; this should be done sparingly owing to the risk of the lubricant finding its way on to the contact points. It is a good plan at this stage to separate the points by pulling the moving arm back with the tip of the finger. The points should have a grey, frosted appearance; they should not be unduly burnt or pitted, although the formation of a slight "pip" on one point and a corresponding crater on the other point is quite normal. Full information regarding servicing the points will be found in Chapter 5.

Sparking Plugs. After 3,000 miles (in addition to the regular 6,000-mile service) it is advisable to remove the sparking plugs and check the gap. This should be 0·028 in. (0·7 mm).

Automatic Cooling Air Intake. On the 1200 and 1300 engine the flow of cooling air through the fan is regulated by a throttle ring at the centre of the fan housing. This ring is linked by an operating lever and a rod to a thermostat which responds to engine temperature. If the lever is incorrectly set, the ring will open too soon, causing the engine to warm up too slowly; or the valve may not open far enough, resulting in overheating. If the ring should open too far it may catch the fan blades, causing considerable noise.

The ring should, therefore, be checked regularly to make sure that when the engine is cold, it is pressing lightly against the air intake flange. When the engine is thoroughly warmed up, the distance between the upper edge of the intake flange and the edge of the throttle ring should be about

1–1¼ in. (25·4–31·8 mm). If the adjustment is incorrect, warm up the engine until the upper end of the thermostat touches the stop on the support in the right-hand lower heater channel, unhook the throttle ring return spring, loosen the operating lever and adjust the ring so that it opens to the extent of 1 in. (25·4 mm). After tightening the operating lever, reconnect the return spring and check the intake for correct operation.

Generator. The bearings of the generator are packed with lubricant on assembly and should require no attention in the ordinary way.

The generator and fan driving belt should be tested and the tension

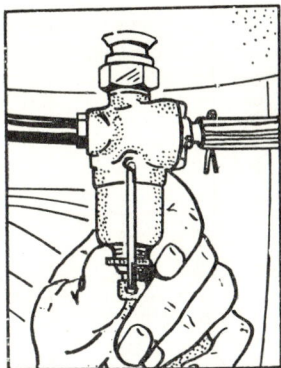

FIG. 14. FUEL FILTER INCOR-
PORATED WITH PETROL TAP
ON EARLY MODELS

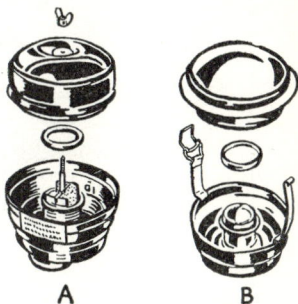

FIG. 15. OIL-BATH AIR CLEANERS
A. Early models
B. Later design

adjusted if required. A slack belt will cause overheating and a low charging rate, whereas too tight a belt overloads the generator and fan shaft bearings. The belt tension is adjusted by altering the position of the spacer washers fitted between the two halves of the driving pulley, as shown in Fig. 16.

To loosen or tighten the nuts on 1200 and 1300 models, use a box spanner on the generator pulley nut and prevent the pulley from turning by inserting a screwdriver in the slot in the half of the pulley nearest the generator, resting the screwdriver against the upper generator housing screw.

On the 1500, 1500S and 1600 engines, the intake housing cover must be removed and the nut on the pulley slackened by using a 21 mm and a 27 mm wrench, applying pressure to the two spanners in opposite directions.

From August 1959 onwards, special heat-resisting fan belts were fitted as standard and these can be used as replacements on earlier cars. They have a longer life and a better resistance to dirt, heat and moisture than the standard type. When installing a belt of this type, from 5 to 8 shims should be fitted between the halves of the pulley. This will give a higher

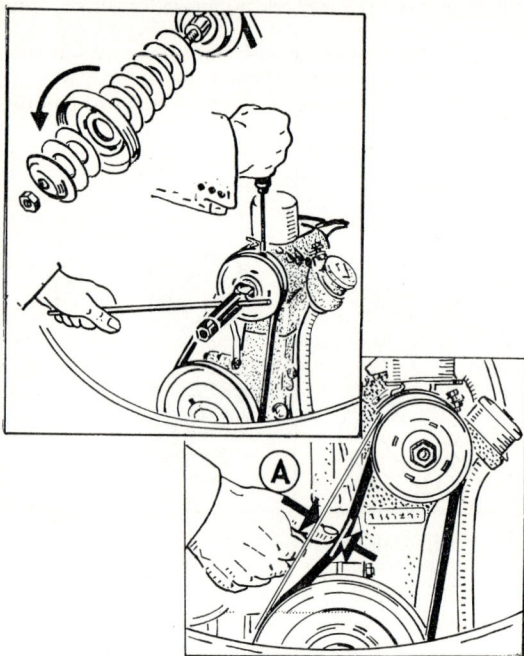

FIG. 16. ADJUSTING THE FAN BELT TENSION

Shims must be transferred to reduce the distance between the pulley flanges. The free movement of the belt *A* (which is exaggerated in the lower sketch), should be approximately ½–¾ in. (12·7–19 mm).

belt tension than normal, but after about 50 miles of running the belt will have stretched sufficiently to restore the normal tension. It is always advisable, however, to check the tension of the belt after 500 miles of use.

Clutch Adjustment. There should be a free movement of between ½–¾ in. (12·7–19 mm) at the clutch pedal. This can be detected by pressing the pedal downwards by hand for a short distance until the full strength of the clutch-engagement springs is felt. If a practice is made of driving with the foot resting on the clutch pedal, excessive wear of the carbon thrust ring in the clutch release mechanism will occur and the pedal travel will become too great. Eventually it may not be possible to release the clutch fully before the pedal reaches the limit of its travel.

If, on the other hand, a driver persistently slips the clutch in order to ease the load on the engine and thus avoid changing to a lower gear, the clutch linings will wear rapidly and the free movement of the pedal will be taken up. Either state of affairs is likely to develop, of course, as a result of normal wear over a fairly large mileage so that an occasional check on the clutch pedal movement is required.

Adjustment is made at the clutch end of the operating cable. On earlier models, the adjusting-nut is locked by a locknut. When this has been slackened the adjusting-nut should be screwed along the threaded cable end until the correct free movement at the pedal is obtained. On late cars, the adjusting-nut has two projections which drop into depressions in the clutch operating lever and is thus self-locking at each half-turn. Lubricate the bearing point between the operating lever and adjusting nut with lithium-base grease.

After adjusting the clutch, operate the pedal quickly several times through its full travel. If excessive free play has again developed, the indication is that the cable is fraying and should be replaced as soon as possible. This is a fairly straightforward job but you may prefer to leave it to a VW agent.

If correct adjustment of the free movement of the pedal fails to restore satisfactory clutch operation, the trouble lies either in a distorted driven plate, damaged or worn linings or grease or oil on the linings. It will be necessary to dismantle the clutch in order to enable the defective parts to be replaced. This job is normally beyond the scope of the average owner.

Steering Gearbox. The steering gearbox must be lubricated only with hypoid gear oil. Grease or ordinary oil (sometimes recommended for certain present-day steering gearboxes) should not be used. The gearbox filler plug is accessible through an inspection opening beneath the spare wheel. The level should be just below the base of the filler plug hole. This attention is not required on later models.

Hydraulic Brake Reservoir. The reservoir for the hydraulic brake fluid (on de luxe and convertible models) is in the front luggage compartment behind the spare wheel. On the Transporter range it is reached by lifting the inspection plate in the floor of the driver's compartment. The reservoir must be kept at least three-quarters full of V.W. Brake Fluid or Lockheed Brake Fluid. *Never top-up with oil.*

Lubricating Brake Cables. When hydraulic brakes are fitted, lubrication is confined to the two rear brake cable conduits and this is only necessary on vehicles up to chassis No. 4,036,536. Only anti-freezing, water-repellent grease should be used, any of the brands listed in Chapter 1 being suitable for the purpose. If lubrication is neglected, there is a possibility of the brakes binding and causing overheating of the shoes and drums, rapid wear of the linings and heavy fuel consumption.

When a mechanical braking system is fitted, lubrication is even more important, since the braking efficiency depends on free movement of the brake cables within the conduits. At the beginning of the winter it is advisable to take the car to a VW service station in order to have the conduit tubes completely filled with grease. Since this entails unhooking the brake cables, withdrawing the footbrake push bar and using a specially-designed lubricating fitting to fill the tubes with grease without removing the cables, it is not a job that the owner should ordinarily tackle.

Valve Clearances. The engine valve clearances should be checked and, if necessary, adjusted as described in Chapter 3.

Minor Lubrication Points. Attention to various small bearings and rubbing surfaces with an oil can or a smear of grease will prolong the life of the parts and prevent rattles developing. For example, the door lock striker plates should be lightly greased, although an excess of lubricant should be avoided owing to the risk of it being transferred to the driver's or passengers' clothes. A few drops of oil should be applied to the door hinges, after removing any dust that has accumulated. On a convertible, the door hinges are provided with lubrication fittings, to which the grease gun can be applied, wiping off any surplus grease afterwards. The door cylinder locks should be treated only with graphite. A small quantity of powdered graphite should be blown through the key hole and the keys should be dipped in graphite, inserted and turned backwards and forwards several times.

The upper and lower sliding surfaces of the seat runners should be lightly greased, after sliding the seat fully forward towards the front. When installing the seat, hook the spring into position.

On a convertible hood there are a number of linkage points which require a few drops of oil. Care must be taken not to allow the oil to stain the top cover, as besides being unsightly, the oil has a detrimental effect on the rubber lining.

The window-regulating mechanism will benefit from occasional lubrication but in order to do this it is necessary to take off the inside door handles and the trim panels. The escutcheon plate on each handle should be pressed down, revealing the securing pin, which can then be pushed out with a suitable small-diameter tool. The trim panel is secured by snap fasteners, which must be gently levered away with a screwdriver, taking care not to scratch the paint or distort the panel. If the novice has any doubts regarding his ability to carry out the work without damaging the panels, it would probably be better to leave the job to a VW dealer.

Changing the Wheels Around. If cross-ply tyres are fitted, it is best, in order to equalize tyre wear as far as possible, to change the wheels around at, say, 3,000-mile intervals, preferably bringing the spare wheel into use if it has a new or slightly-worn tyre. The spare wheel should be fitted to the nearside front hub.

When radial-ply tyres are used, however, it is better not to change the wheels around. The tyres on the front and rear wheels develop different tread profiles as they wear and the steering and roadholding can be upset if the wheels are interchanged.

Cleaning Oil Filter. Dealing first with all models except the 411 range, the only oil filter provided takes the form of an inverted gauze cup which is retained by a pressed steel plate at the centre of the sump. Before the plate is removed it will, of course, be necessary to drain the engine oil. The nuts securing the oil filter retaining plate will be more accessible if the rear of the car is first raised. It is a good plan to run the car on to a pair of steel ramps, such as the excellent H.E. car ramps, obtainable from the Hanstock Engineering Co., Blyth Rd., Maltby, Rotherham, Yorks. Propping up the car on makeshift piles of bricks is a dangerous practice and well-designed portable ramps are worth their weight in gold (but quite inexpensive) to the practical owner!

When the bottom plate has been removed the filter can be withdrawn. It should be brushed out with clean paraffin. When it is reassembled, new gaskets should be fitted and the flanges should be scraped clean to prevent oil leaks. The filter should fit snugly around the oil intake pipe.

When the filter has been removed and refitted once or twice the flange may become distorted, owing to the retaining nuts having been over-tightened. Oil leakage past the flange can usually be cured, however, by fitting an extra gasket between the plate and the filter flange—that is, by using three gaskets (one above and two below the filter flange) instead of the two normally fitted.

An improved type of oil filter fitted to later models has a magnetic filter element that is fitted to the centre of the oil filter retaining plate so that it embraces the oil suction pipe. After the oil has passed through the normal gauze strainer it enters the magnetic filter, which removes any iron particles that may be carried in suspension in the oil. In practice, the magnetic filter also arrests non-ferrous particles and carbon deposits which are carried along with the iron particles. The magnetic filter is, therefore, a very worthwhile modification and can be obtained from VW dealers.

Changing the Oil Filter on 411, 411L, 411E and 411LE Models. At every second oil change—that is, normally at 6,000-mile intervals—the full-flow oil filter fitted to the VW411, 411L, 411E and 411LE should be unscrewed and discarded and a new filter should be fitted. This must be done in addition to removing and cleaning the oil strainer, which is similar to that on earlier engines but is retained by a single nut. New gaskets and washers must be used when refitting the filter plate and the retaining nut should, ideally, be tightened with a torque-wrench to a torque of 7–9 lb ft (1–1·3 mkg).

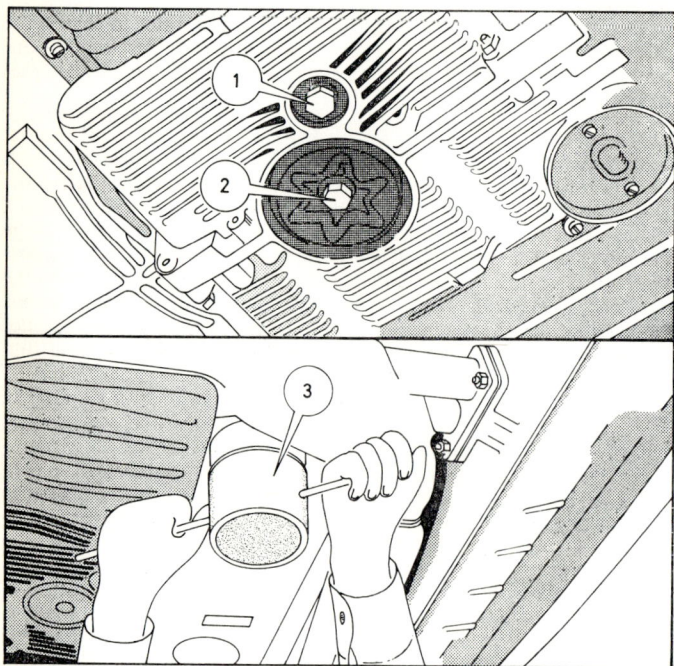

FIG. 17. THE UNDERSIDE OF THE ENGINE OF THE 411 and 411E MODELS

The engine-oil drain plug is shown at 1, and the nut which retains the oil strainer at 2. A special tool, 3, is needed to remove the oil filter cartridge.

A special tubular wrench is needed to unscrew the cartridge filter, which is reached from beneath the car, and to fit the replacement. It should be possible to obtain this tool from a VW dealer—but you may, of course, decide to allow him to carry out the whole of the somewhat messy business of cleaning the strainer and renewing the filter.

Lubricating Gear Lever. If the gear lever becomes stiff, it can be lubricated after it has been removed by withdrawing the two screws that attach the dome to the tunnel. The lever, dome and spring can then be lifted away as one unit. The bearing surfaces in the dome, at the stop-plate and the lever ball socket, should be well smeared with grease. When installing the stop-plate, care should be taken that the turned-up edge is on the right-hand side. After installation, make sure that the gears are selected correctly. If necessary, remove the gear lever and re-position it to obtain correct selection.

General Check-over. During the 6,000-mile service the engine, transmission and drive casings should be inspected for oil leaks. They should be cleaned down with paraffin, since it is difficult to detect the source of

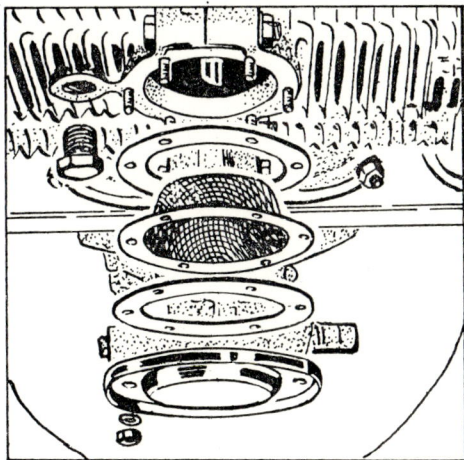

FIG. 18. REMOVING ENGINE OIL FILTER FOR CLEANING

The sump drain plug is to the left of the filter, as shown, on earlier models. On later engines it is at the centre of the filter plate as shown in Fig. 17.

a leak when the parts are covered with oil, dust and mud. The action of the automatic cooling air control should be checked, preferably by a VW dealer. Also, ask your dealer to check over the exhaust, carburettor, intake manifold and fuel pump flange bolts and nuts. While he is carrying out this work he can put the car on a lift and check over the chassis, body, front axle, rear axle, and steering components.

Checking Oil Level in Transmission. When a manually-controlled

transmission is fitted, the oil level can be checked by removing the combined oil filler and level plug from the side of the transmission casing
(indicated in Figs. 11, 12 and 19), and injecting oil until it begins to
dribble out of the filler hole, as described in the next section, which deals
with changing the transmission oil.

When a fully-automatic transmission is fitted, the fluid level can be
checked with the combined filler and dipstick, which is located at the
front edge of the engine compartment. The engine must be idling, with
the selector lever at N, and the transmission oil must be fully warmed-up.

As the correct oil level is vital for proper operation of the transmission,
it must be checked very carefully. Wipe the dipstick with a lint-free cloth
before taking the reading. The level must be between the two marks at
the end of the dipstick—never, in any circumstances, below the lower
mark or above the upper mark.

Before inserting the dipstick, make sure that the ring-shaped handle is
vertical; otherwise trouble will be experienced with the transmission. It
is worth remembering that the difference between the upper and lower
marks is less than ¾ pint (0·4 litre). If the transmission should be over-
filled, the surplus must be drained off. The best method of topping-up is
to use a clean funnel with a plastic extension tube pushed over the end.

Changing Transmission Oil. At 30,000 miles the oil in the transmission
and the differential of a manual transmission should be drained and
replaced by fresh oil of the correct grade. This job is best left to your VW
dealer since the filler plug in the transmission casing is somewhat in-
accessible and the easiest method of refilling the casing is with the aid of
an injector gun with a right-angled nozzle. On early cars, however, the
filler orifice faces upwards and it is possible to pour the oil in with the aid
of a suitable funnel; but the VW dealer prefers to work from below. Also,
on later models the drain plugs have recessed heads, calling for the use of
a special spanner which can be obtained from the VW dealers.

The oil sometimes runs into the transmission casing very slowly. If any
attempt is made to hurry the refilling, the oil may overflow and give the
impression that the correct level has been reached, although in fact only
2–3 pints (1–1·5 litres) have been put in.

On the Transporter, each rear wheel reduction gear must be drained
and refilled at the same intervals as the transmission casing

On later cars and Transporters (from 1960) magnetic drain plugs are
fitted to the transmission and reduction gear casings. These should be
checked for the presence of metallic dust or chips (which would indicate
possible trouble) whenever the oil is changed and also at 3,000-mile
intervals. To carry out the latter inspection without draining the casings,
have ready a spare plug or a cork which can be used to block the drain hole.

If magnetic plugs are not fitted as standard, substitution of the later
plugs is a worthwhile modification.

When a fully-automatic transmission is fitted, it must be drained and refilled after 30,000 miles (50,000 kilometres), but if the car has been operating under fairly strenuous conditions—for example, towing a trailer, or if a high proportion of driving is done in city traffic—it is advisable to change the fluid after 18,000 miles (30,000 kilometres).

The drain plug is in the side of the pressed-steel oil pan. After draining the fluid, which will be very hot if the car has been run for some distance, the oil pan and strainer must be taken off and cleaned. A new gasket must be used when refitting the oil pan and a torque wrench is needed to

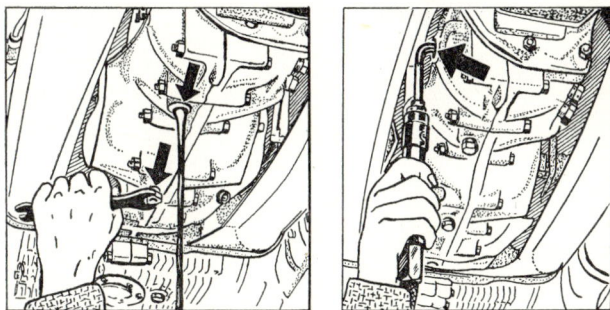

FIG. 19. DRAINING THE TRANSMISSION OIL

It will be necessary to remove two plugs. On later engines a special wrench is needed to fit the recessed drain plugs. A special oil injector (*right*) simplifies refilling the transmission from below

tighten the oil-pan screw to 7 lb/ft (1 mkg), in order to prevent distortion of the flange of the pan. Since the new gasket will settle-down, the screws must again be tightened two or three times at intervals of about five minutes, to the same torque figure. Another job best done by your VW dealer?

When refilling the transmission, first pour in about 4½ pints (2·5 litres) of the correct automatic transmission fluid, start the engine and, with the car stationary, move the selector lever to each position in turn to fill the system. Then, with the selector lever at *N*, check the level with the dipstick. The fluid should be up to the tip of the dipstick at this stage. If necessary, add sufficient fluid to bring it to this level. Then take the car for a run to warm-up the transmission and finally restore the correct level as described on page 46.

With a fully-automatic transmission, the oil in the final-drive is not changed. The level should, however, be checked by removing the filler plug in the side of the transmission casing. It should be level with the lower edge of the hole.

Front Wheel Bearings. When the car leaves the factory, the front wheel bearings are packed with sufficient grease to last for at least 30,000 miles. The caps that seal the front wheel hubs should not be filled with grease. After 30,000 miles have been covered, the bearings should be dismantled as described in Chapter 8, cleaned, inspected and repacked with four ounces of grease for each wheel. The ball bearings should first be filled and the remaining grease applied to the brake drum hub. Finally, the front wheel bearings must be carefully adjusted. As is stressed in Chapter 8, this job should preferably be carried out by a VW dealer who is thoroughly familiar with the correct adjustment of the bearings—a vital point if rapid bearing wear is to be avoided.

3 Engine servicing and tuning

DECARBONIZING

DECARBONIZING is not a job that would normally be tackled by the average owner, since it is necessary to remove the engine in order to carry out the work effectively. Although, on early cars, it is possible to decarbonize with the engine in place, more effective results will be obtained by removing the engine and stripping it on the bench. In the circumstances, therefore, it is as well to consult your VW dealer when decarbonizing is thought to be required.

It should be remembered that, although the term "decarbonizing" is usually applied to the work, in practice the operation would be better described as a top overhaul, since it is advisable to remove and grind-in valves at the same time. On VW engines it is also a relatively simple matter to remove the cylinder barrels at this stage to allow the piston rings and cylinders to be inspected and new rings to be fitted if necessary.

There are several methods of removing carbon which can be employed without taking off the cylinder-heads, including the use of chemical decarbonizers, scouring of the combustion chambers with crushed vegetable grit blown in through the sparking plug holes by using a compressed air blast and a special gun, and the use of an oxygen flame. Although the carbon may be removed quite efficiently by these methods, the valves and valve seats receive no attention—and it is nearly always essential to recondition these vital items if engine performance is to be restored.

How Often is Decarbonizing Required? It is difficult to answer this question in terms of mileage alone, since driving methods, the qualities of fuel and lubricating oil used and the mechanical condition of the engine can vary so widely, and all these factors affect the rate at which carbon is deposited. Some authorities recommend that the cylinder head of a modern car should be removed after the first 5,000 miles have been covered, so that the valves can be lightly ground-in to counteract any slight distortion that may have occurred during the initial "stabilizing" period. Stresses set up in the engine components during manufacture will have been relieved after this mileage has been covered and further attention can be deferred until a considerably greater additional mileage (say 15,000–20,000 miles) has been covered.

In general, the need for decarbonization is indicated by progressive

49

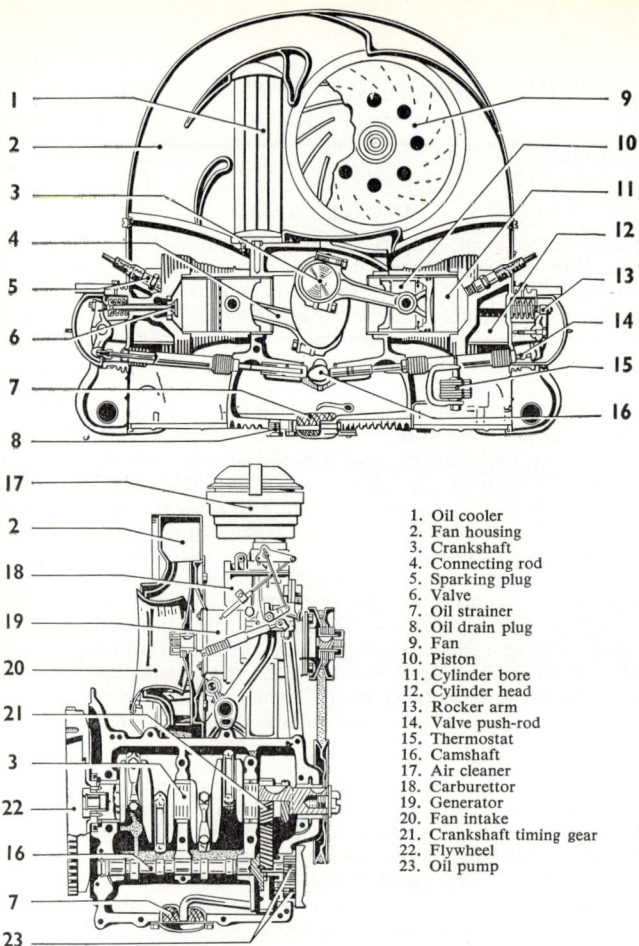

1. Oil cooler
2. Fan housing
3. Crankshaft
4. Connecting rod
5. Sparking plug
6. Valve
7. Oil strainer
8. Oil drain plug
9. Fan
10. Piston
11. Cylinder bore
12. Cylinder head
13. Rocker arm
14. Valve push-rod
15. Thermostat
16. Camshaft
17. Air cleaner
18. Carburettor
19. Generator
20. Fan intake
21. Crankshaft timing gear
22. Flywheel
23. Oil pump

FIG. 20. SECTIONS THROUGH THE VW 1200 ENGINE

This cross-section is typical of the range of models, although minor differences are found in early and later engines. See Figs. 1 and 21.

deterioration in performance, sometimes accompanied by a tendency or the engine to overheat and for "pinking" to occur at low speeds in top great together with symptoms of pre-ignition and a tendency for the engine to run-on when the ignition is switched off. These symptoms are pointers to the need for the relatively simple job involved in a systematic top-overhaul of the engine.

Perhaps, at this stage, the term "pinking" should be explained. Modern

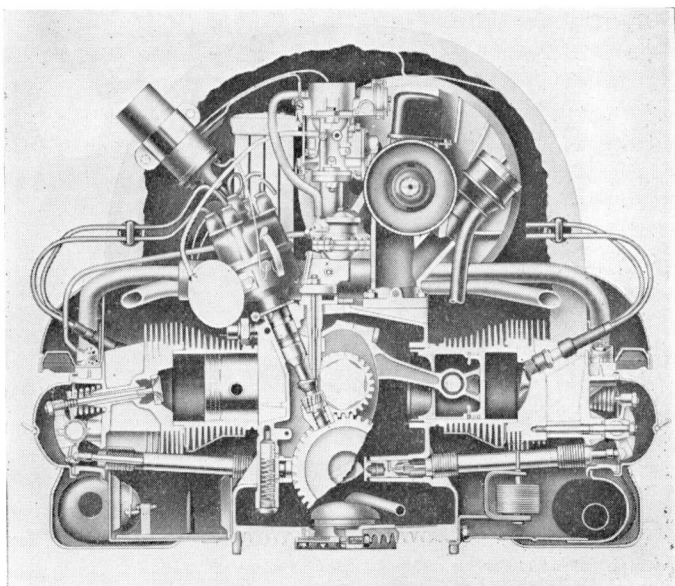

FIG. 21. THE LATER 40 B.H.P. ENGINE

premium fuels have such high octane numbers (or anti-knock properties) that "pinking," the light metallic tinkling or knocking sound hearb when the engine is pulling hard, can virtually be eliminated, even though the engine may contain heavy carbon deposits. At intervals of, say, 5,000 miles, therefore, the level of petrol in the tank should be allowed to fall as low as is prudent and the tank should be filled with a standard grade of petrol instead of a premium fuel. Even a trace of premium fuel in the tank will tend to suppress "pinking," so it is best to use the first tankful and then to fill again with standard petrol.

At this stage "pinking" should be evident, even in a clean engine, provided that the ignition is correctly set. It should be apparent, however, only when the engine is pulling hard in top gear and should normally become inaudible before 30 m.p.h. is reached. If the engine continues to "pink" at higher speeds, either the ignition is over-advanced or the combustion chambers have acquired an excessive deposit of carbon, which has raised the compression ratio of the engine.

A further point is that the presence of carbon deposits can also cause

FIG. 22. THE COMPACT ENGINE OF THE 1500S

The 1600 engine is very similar (see Fig. 4). The 1500 power unit is basically the same but has only one carburettor.

1. Exhaust silencer	7. Crankshaft
2. Cooling-air duct	8. Clutch and flywheel
3. Cooling-fan intake	9. Interior-heater air duct
4. Ignition coil	10. Valve gear
5. Carburettor	11. Heat-exchanger for interior heater
6. Air cleaner and silencer	

pre-ignition, owing to particles of carbon becoming incandescent and firing the mixture prematurely; that is, before the instant at which the spark normally occurs at the plug points. This will cause rough running and will aggravate "pinking." It may also cause the engine to back-fire or to run-on for several seconds after the ignition has been switched off.

It is possible to delay the point at which decarbonization is necessary by slightly retarding the ignition, as described in Chapter 5, but this should be regarded purely as a temporary measure. The engine should be decarbonized and the valves should be ground-in as soon as possible.

Reduced compression in one or more cylinders is, however, the main fault that renders a top-overhaul imperative. The best plan is to have the compression of each cylinder accurately measured by a compression gauge at, say, 10,000-mile intervals; VW agents have the necessary equipment. If the compression is weak on one or more cylinders the most likely cause is burnt or pitted valve faces. Leakage of gases past the piston rings cannot, of course, be discounted but this fault will normally be accompanied also by excessive oil consumption.

To conclude this brief summary of a somewhat complex subject, it should be recorded that most car manufacturers recommend that the engine of a car in the "family" class is best left undisturbed provided that it is running satisfactorily. There is little object in removing the cylinder-heads at any arbitrary mileage—say, 10,000 miles—as was once recommended, simply in order to inspect the valves and the condition of the combustion chambers.

Carbon formation can also be reduced by fitting efficient atomizers in the inlet manifold or manifolds (see page 63).

VALVES

Checking the Valve Clearance. It is essential to maintain the correct clearance between the valve-operating rockers and the ends of the valve stems. If the clearance is too great, the valve timing will be affected and performance will suffer. Similarly, too small a clearance will also affect the valve timing and may cause burning of the valve seatings and faces, owing to the risk of the valve being held partly off its seating.

As the correct clearance differs for various engines, and in some cases differs also for the inlet and exhaust valves, it is essential to set the clearances to the figures given in Chapter 1. In all cases the clearances should be measured with the engine cold.

In order to obtain access to the valve rockers, the valve covers must be removed after springing aside the retaining clips.

The cylinders can be quickly identified, if it is remembered that they are numbered as follows: No. 1, right front. No. 2, right rear. No. 3, left front. No. 4, left rear. The front of the engine is the flywheel end; that is, the cylinders are regarded as being viewed from the rear of the car. Adjustment should be carried out in the following sequence: 1st, 2nd, 3rd, and 4th cylinder.

The valves should be adjusted when the piston of the corresponding cylinder is at top-dead-centre on the compression stroke. With the sparking plugs removed, starting with the first cylinder, crank the engine over slowly in an anti-clockwise direction by applying a spanner to the generator pulley nut, with the distributor cap removed. On the 1500, 1500S and 1600 models it will also be necessary to remove the intake housing cover.

Bring the distributor rotor arm into line with the No. 1 cylinder mark on the rim of the distributor and check the clearance between the tip of each rocker and the end of each valve of No. 1 cylinder. If the clearance is incorrect, loosen the adjusting screw lock-nuts and re-set the clearance by turning the adjusting screws. Tighten each lock-nut and re-check the clearances. Then turn the engine anti-clockwise until the rotor arm has moved through 90° and check and if necessary adjust the clearances of No. 2 cylinder. Again turn the engine until the rotor has moved through

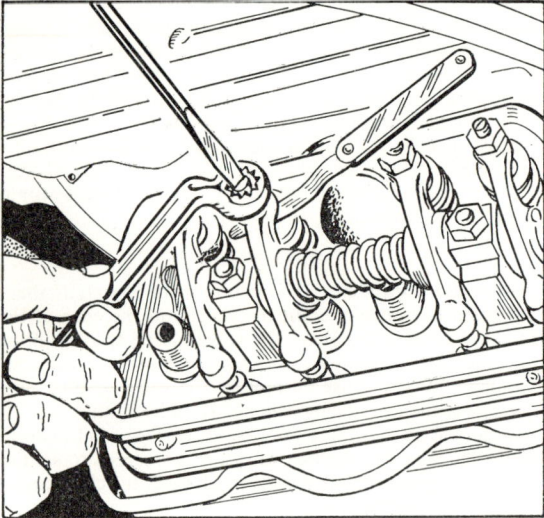

FIG. 23. ADJUSTING THE TAPPETS

90°, check the clearances for No. 3 cylinder and finally turn the rotor through another 90° to allow the clearances of No. 4 cylinder to be checked.

Positioning Valve Rockers. An important point to check, if the valve rocker shaft has been removed for any reason, is that the ball-ends of the push-rods rest centrally in the sockets of the rocker arms and that the tips of the valve clearance adjusting screws do *not* bear on the centres of the valve stems. They should be slightly offset by an amount equal to half the radius of the stem. In other words, while not being central, they should not be offset towards the extreme edge of the valve stem but should take up a position midway between these two points. This will impart a rotary action to the valves which will reduce the wear on the valve stems, facings and seatings.

The correct position can be obtained by moving the rocker-arm shaft sideways in its clearance holes for the studs before tightening the retaining nuts. It may be necessary to alter the length of the rocker-arm spacers or the thickness of the washers, or to fit additional washers, if the correct setting has been disturbed at some previous dismantling.

ENGINE TUNING

No one, even by the wildest stretch of imagination, would have suggested that when Dr. Porsche designed the Volkswagen, he intended to confer on it the liveliness and handling characteristics of a sports car. Essentially the VW was intended as an economical means of family transport, combining low running and maintenance costs with exceptional standards of reliability and a very long life between overhauls.

Why is it, then, that even experienced sports-car drivers become enthusiastic over the handling of the Volkswagen? Undoubtedly one of the chief factors is the effortless cruising at speeds in the sixties conferred by the relatively high top-gear ratio. At 60 m.p.h. the engine is running at less than 3,000 r.p.m. and the pistons are travelling at about 1,250 f.p.m., or less than half the speed normally regarded as a desirable maximum by engine designers.

Naturally, the high top-gear ratio does not permit outstanding acceleration in this gear; it is essentially a cruising ratio, similar to an overdrive on more conventionally-geared cars. Even when third gear is engaged, however, the engine revolutions do not exceed 4,500 r.p.m. at 60 m.p.h.—and this again is quite a conservative figure by modern standards. Moreover, third gear enables 30 m.p.h. to be reached from 10 m.p.h. in half the time required when top gear is engaged and a similar improvement applies in the 20–40 m.p.h. and 30–50 m.p.h. ranges.

In its standard form, therefore, the VW saloon or convertible provides all the performance that the average owner is likely to require, coupled, of course, with an excellent fuel consumption which is unlikely to fall below 30–35 m.p.g. even when the car is driven really hard, and which should be in the neighbourhood of 38 m.p.g. when more gentle driving is the order of the day.

There will always be a proportion of owners, however, who desire that little extra performance which sets their car apart from the general run of standard models and who are prepared to pay a moderate penalty in terms of the cost of conversion, and even to sacrifice a certain amount of fuel economy if full advantage is taken of the increased performance What can be done in this respect where the VW is concerned?

First it can be said that the engine is capable of being tuned quite effectively without the loss of reliability; moreover, the increased efficiency of the engine in modified form compensates to a large degree for any loss in fuel economy. In other words, one can obtain substantially increased performance without paying too dearly for the privilege.

It is never wise for the amateur to attempt major modifications to an engine, however, unless he possesses a fully-equipped workshop and—more important still—has sufficient knowledge and experience to be able to forecast the results of his efforts. Preferably it should be possible to assess the effects of each stage of tuning by running the engine under controlled conditions on a test bench; moreover, the possible effect of the modifications on the all-important question of reliability must be carefully weighed-up.

It is always best, therefore, to put such work in the hands of a specialist. British owners would be well advised to get into touch with Speedwell Performance Conversions Ltd., 260 Berkhampstead Road, Chesham, Bucks. In conjunction with Engineered Motor Products Inc. in the United States of America, the British company produces or markets a wide range of "go faster" kits for the VW. A Stage 1 conversion for the 1200 and 1300 engine, for example, consists of two Stromberg carburettors, fitted to short inlet manifolds, which give a considerable increase in performance without jeopardizing the reliability of the engine. More advanced tuning stages are also available, including special kits which increase the capacity of the engine to 1,600 c.c.

An entirely different approach to the question of engine tuning is to fit a supercharger kit. This may well be the ideal solution, in fact, for an owner who has not the facilities to remove and strip the engine in order to incorporate the fairly expensive modifications which are necessary to ensure a reasonable increase in power output.

A modern low-pressure supercharger kit consists of all the necessary parts to enable a belt-driven supercharger to be bolted to the inlet manifold in place of the carburettor, the carburettor in turn being attached to an intake flange on the supercharger. It is necessary only to remove the air cleaner, fuel pipe, ignition vacuum control pipe and the carburettor from the engine. A driving pulley is installed on the end of the crankshaft in front of the fan pulley and an automatic lubricator is attached to the engine bulkhead. The supercharger can then be fitted, the carburettor attached to it and the pipe lines and throttle linkage connected up. A different jet is fitted in the carburettor.

The whole process can be completed in a morning or afternoon.

Owing to the fact that a full charge is forced into the cylinders under all normal conditions, plus about one-third of the capacity of each cylinder when the engine is operating at full power, a supercharger transforms the performance of the car. Liveliness, top speed and pulling power are all greatly improved. The time taken to reach 50 m.p.h. from a standstill can be almost halved and maximum speed is increased by about 10 m.p.h.

Naturally, if full use is made of the improved performance, some reduction in fuel consumption must be expected, but under ordinary running conditions the adverse balance should not exceed 5–10 per cent. When a supercharged engine is driven gently, it will often return better consumption figures than when unsupercharged, owing to better atomization of the fuel and improved distribution to the cylinders.

A low-pressure supercharger of the type just described should not be confused with the higher-pressure units used in the past on racing cars, but it is advisable to contact your insurance company before installing

FIG. 24. NEAT INSTALLATION OF A PECO-JUDSON SUPERCHARGER ON AN OTHERWISE UNMODIFIED 1200 ENGINE

the supercharger as an increased premium may be imposed on the supercharged vehicle.

The supercharger requires no maintenance or attention over very long mileages, apart from topping up the oil reservoir. The kit illustrated in Fig. 24 is the Judson installation, an American supercharger which has been fitted to a very large number of Volkswagens. It is handled in Great Britain and Ireland by the Performance Equipment Co. Ltd., Sandford Street, Birkenhead, Cheshire. The Shorrock supercharger conversion kit also gives excellent results. Details can be obtained from Shorrock Superchargers Ltd., Church Hill, Wednesbury, Staffs.

4 Fuel system and carburation

When difficult starting, misfiring and loss of power are experienced, many owners automatically blame the carburettor, or the fuel injection system, in the case of the 411E models. Similarly, when the petrol consumption of a car begins to increase—probably after the vehicle has covered many thousands of miles—the owner is apt to believe that a mysterious process known as "tuning the carburettor" is the magic key to restoring the original performance and economy.

Experience has shown, however, that the carburettor or fuel system is the major culprit only in comparatively few cases. Other faults, such as ignition system troubles, badly-seating valves, worn piston rings and cylinders, leaking cylinder-head gaskets, defective inlet manifold or carburettor gaskets and even binding brakes, will adversely affect performance and fuel consumption; some can also contribute very substantially to difficult starting.

Before blaming the carburettor, therefore, the mechanical condition of the engine and the car as a whole should be carefully checked. Your VW dealer has the necessary equipment to carry out such work quickly and efficiently and it should not be necessary to stress the value of expert opinion in cases of this nature. When discussing faults such as difficult starting and excessive fuel consumption in this chapter, therefore, it will be assumed that these preliminary checks have been carried out.

If the simple maintenance described in this chapter is conscientiously followed, carburettor and fuel system faults should seldom be experienced. It should be emphasized that the carburettor itself does not "wear out," in the general sense of the words, during the normal life of a car. Apart from the throttle spindle bearings there are virtually no wearing parts in the carburettor in the accepted sense.

What has been said so far regarding carburation applies with even greater emphasis to the fuel-injection system fitted to the 411E models and described on pages 69–71. Fault-tracing or adjustments to this electronically-controlled system are the province of the VW dealer.

THE CARBURETTOR

Fuel is fed from the rear tank by a mechanical petrol pump which supplies the Solex carburettor. Although the carburettor might appear, from a reference to Figs. 25–31, to be a somewhat complex instrument it is, in fact, quite straightforward and maintenance and adjustment are well within the scope of the average owner.

Settings that differ from standard may be necessary in countries in which there is any marked difference in the type of petrol available, in

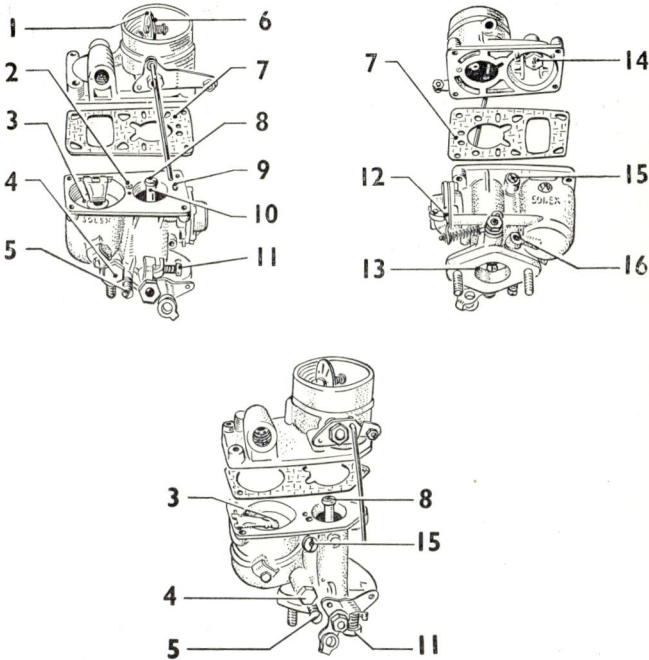

FIG. 25. THE CARBURETTOR FITTED TO CARS BEFORE AUGUST 1960 AND TO UTILITY VEHICLES BEFORE MAY 1959

(*Upper, left and right*) carburettor fitted to later cars. (*Lower*) the carburettor fitted to early models, without accelerator pump

1. Choke
2. Pilot jet air bleed
3. Float
4. Main jet
5. Volume control screw
6. Poppet valve
7. Gasket
8. Air correction jet
9. Pump pipe fitting
10. Emulsion tube
11. Throttle stop screw
12. Accelerator pump
13. Throttle
14. Float needle-valve
15. Pilot jet
16. Vacuum pipe connexion

atmospheric conditions or in the altitudes at which the car is normally operated. In such cases the advice of the local VW agent should be sought.

When the car is operated at high altitudes, an altitude corrector can be fitted in place of the main jet, in order to provide a suitable mixture strength. Consisting of a main jet holder with jet and jet needle which is automatically operated by means of a bellows which responds to changes in atmospheric pressure, the corrector can be installed without difficulty.

A modified type of carburettor is fitted to engines installed in utility vehicles after May 1959 and in cars from August 1960 onwards. This carburettor, and later types, has an automatic choke which is controlled, when the starting control is operated, by a bi-metal spring which reacts to outside temperature. Two further refinements are incorporated: an electric heating element, wired to the ignition circuit, which also acts on the spring, and an automatic vacuum control connected to the inlet manifold. This consists of a piston which acts through a lever on the choke valve and prevents the mixture from becoming too rich at higher engine speeds, under light throttle openings, particularly when the car is overrunning the engine.

Another feature which will be found on most of the later types of carburettor is an electro-magnetic valve which controls the flow of fuel to the slow-running jet. This takes its current through the ignition switch and closes whenever the ignition is switched off. By positively shutting off the flow of fuel to the slow-running jet, it prevents any risk of "running-on"—that is, the tendency of an engine to continue to run roughly for several seconds after the ignition has been switched off, which may be caused by local overheating in the combustion chamber, too rich an idling mixture or too high an idling speed. Some fuels are also prone to cause the trouble. Hence the provision of the electro-magnetic shut-off valve, which can be fitted, if required, to a carburettor which is not already so equipped.

On later cars provision is made for supplying warm air to the carburettor at temperatures below 10°C (50°F). This improves fuel consumption and reduces the risk of carburettor-icing in cold, damp weather. On the 1200, 1300 and 1600 models, the weighted flap on the air cleaner must be free to move in cold weather but must be fixed in the open position by wedging the lever under the ridge on the intake pipe, or by using the clip provided, when the average temperature is above 10°C (50°F). On the VW 1500 there are two flaps. The left-hand flap must be free to move but the right-hand flap is thermostatically controlled. The action of the flap or flaps should be checked whenever the air cleaner is cleaned.

It is worth recording that this useful refinement can be fitted to earlier engines, the modification involving only a change of air cleaner.

Carburettor Adjustment. The throttle stop screw controls the amount by which the throttle approaches the closed position and therefore regulates the slow-running speed. The richness of the slow-running mixture is determined by the setting of the volume control screw, a greater volume of petrol being admitted, and the mixture enriched, when the screw is turned anti-clockwise.

To obtain the exact settings the engine should be at normal running temperature and the throttle stop screw set so that the engine runs at a

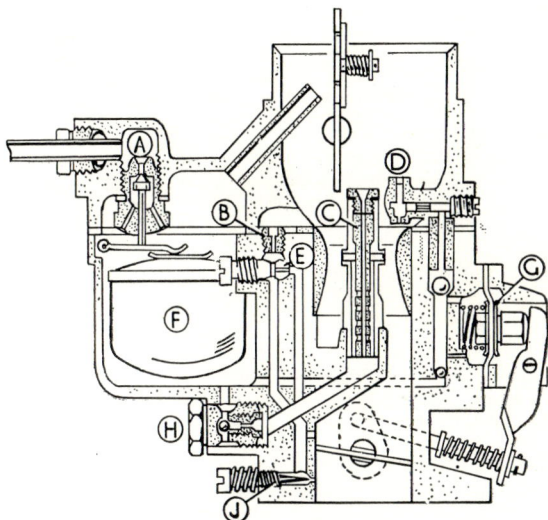

FIG. 26. SECTION THROUGH CARBURETTOR FITTED TO SOME LATER 1200 MODELS

A. Petrol inlet and needle-valve
B. Pilot jet air bleed
C. Emulsifying tube
D. Accelerator pump jet air bleed
E. Pilot jet

F. Float
G. Accelerator pump diaphragm
H. Main jet
J. Mixture volume control screw

fast idling speed. Considering first the single-carburettor engines, the volume control screw should be screwed inwards until it seats lightly and should then be unscrewed by about three-quarters of a turn. This will give an approximate setting on which the engine can be started. The volume control screw should then be turned to enrich or weaken the mixture until the engine is firing evenly. If the mixture is too weak, the engine is likely to stall or spit back in the carburettor when suddenly accelerated and the exhaust will sound irregular and "splashy."

When the volume control is correctly set, the engine may run at a higher

3

speed; it will then be necessary to re-adjust the throttle stop screw, followed by a slight adjustment to the volume control screw.

The strength of the slow-running mixture considerably influences acceleration from low speeds. If there is a "flat spot" when the throttle is opened from the idling position, try the effect of slightly enriching the slow-running mixture; one-sixth of a turn of the screw may be sufficient.

The best setting can be arrived at by taking the car on the road and testing the dead-slow running in first and second gears, followed by the pick-up

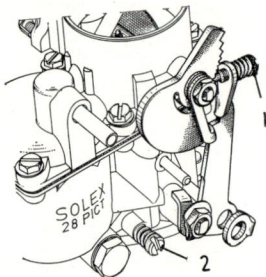

FIG. 27. SLOW-RUNNING ADJUSTMENTS ON THE CARBURETTOR
FITTED TO 1300, 1500 AND LATER 1200 MODELS

1. Idling-speed adjustment 2. Mixture volume-control screw.

from this speed when the throttle is opened. By careful adjustment of the throttle-stop and volume control screws, very smooth acceleration, entirely free from flat spots, can be obtained. It will be found that the final idling mixture setting arrived at in this manner is usually somewhat richer than that obtained when the carburettor is adjusted strictly in accordance with the manufacturer's instruction book.

When twin carburettors are fitted, adjustment calls for more skill, as it is essential to synchronize the throttle opening and the idling mixture setting in both carburettors. This is best done with the special test equipment available at Volkswagen dealers and agents, but if the job must be tackled by the owner the following method will give quite satisfactory results. It is advisable, however, to have the setting checked by a VW agent or dealer as soon as possible.

Starting with the engine warm, unclip the rod which connects the right-hand carburettor to the three-armed lever at the centre of the engine. Unscrew the throttle-stop screws, which adjust the idling speed, on both carburettors until they are clear of the throttle-valve levers and make sure that the throttle valves are fully closed by applying gentle pressure to the throttle levers. Turn each screw clockwise until it just touches the throttle lever and then give each screw a further half-turn.

Start the engine and turn the volume-control screw of one carburettor clockwise until the engine speed begins to drop. Then unscrew the screw a quarter of a turn. Carry out the same adjustment on the second carburettor and then regulate the idling speed to give a fairly fast tick-over, with the generator warning light just fading out, by adjusting the throttle stop screws on both carburettors by an exactly equal amount.

The connecting rod can now be reconnected to the three-arm lever. It

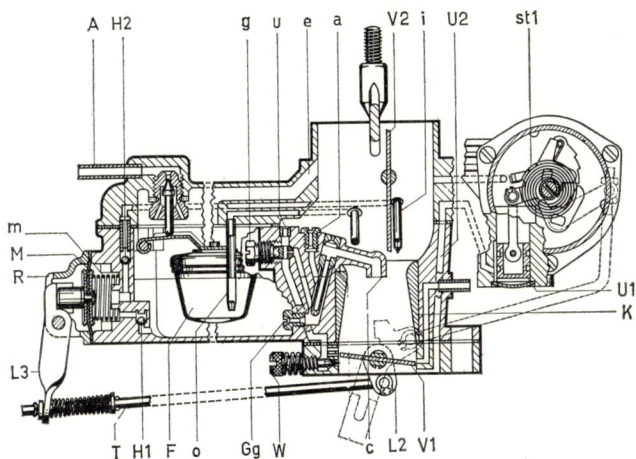

FIG. 28. CARBURETTOR FITTED TO 1500S AND 1600 L AND TL

For key, *see* page 66

should drop into place on the peg without interference. If necessary, adjust the length of the rod by slackening the two lock-nuts and rotating it in the ball joints. Re-tighten the lock-nuts and lubricate the joints in the links sparingly with engine oil.

Inlet Manifold Modifier. A really substantial improvement in engine pulling power and smoothness—particularly at low speeds—combined with reduced petrol consumption, can be obtained by fitting a G.M. inlet manifold modifier between the manifold and the carburettor. The modifier re-atomizes the drops of petrol that condense on the throttle plate and would otherwise run down the walls of the manifolds. Although simple in design and having no moving parts, the modifier is extremely efficient and can be recommended from practical experience. It can be obtained from the G. M. Carburettor Co. Ltd., Malt St., Knutsford, Cheshire. Two modifers will be needed when twin carburettors are fitted.

Difficult Starting. When difficult starting is experienced it should not be assumed that the carburettor is necessarily to blame. Ignition faults are among the most likely causes of this trouble and the ignition system should be systematically checked over as described in Chapter 5. Similarly, the condition of the piston rings and of the engine generally can considerably influence the ease of starting in very cold weather, although such faults may be of relatively little importance during the summer

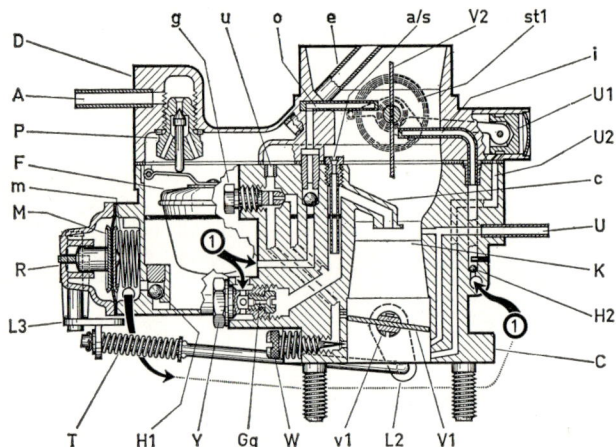

FIG. 29. CARBURETTOR FITTED TO 1300 AND TO SOME LATER 1200 AND 1500 MODELS

For key, *see* page 66

months. Finally, a weak battery or an inefficient starter motor, which fails to rotate the engine at a sufficiently high cranking speed, can render it very difficult indeed to obtain the ideal conditions within the combustion chambers that are necessary to ensure an easy start in freezing weather.

As far as the carburettor is concerned, therefore, attention should be limited to checking the adjustment of the starting control and slow-running adjustments. It should also be verified that the screws retaining the bowl cover are firmly tightened.

Excessive Fuel Consumption. Flooding or too high a petrol level in the float chamber is, of course, one of the most likely causes of excessive fuel consumption. Leakage at any of the joints on the carburettor can also increase fuel consumption by a significant figure. Usually, however, the carburettor is blamed for heavy fuel consumption when the trouble is in fact due to poor mechanical condition of the engine, to ignition faults such as dirty sparking plugs or incorrectly set plug gaps, dirty or pitted contact-breaker points, or to over-retarding of the ignition timing. Binding brakes are another common cause.

A less likely cause of excessive fuel consumption is a worn float chamber needle and seating or a leaking needle-valve washer. This is usually

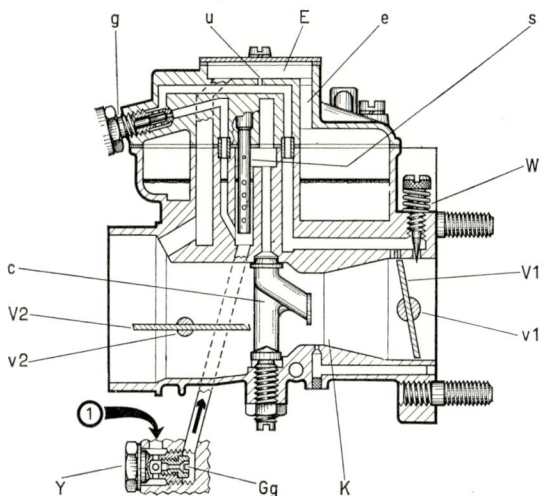

FIG. 30. SECTION THROUGH CARBURETTOR FITTED
TO 1600A AND EARLY 1500 MODELS

This illustrates the electro-magnetic valve g which controls the flow of idling mixture.
The other parts are identified by the key on page 66.

indicated by the fact that it is impossible to obtain a really smooth tick-over, irrespective of the carburettor adjustment. Black smoke will be apparent from the exhaust and when running downhill with the throttle partly closed, petrol fumes may be apparent in the car. The inexpensive remedy for this is to fit a new needle-valve assembly.

Flooding, on the other hand, is sometimes caused by the presence of foreign matter in the needle-valve assembly, although it may possibly be caused by a punctured float. A quick check for the latter trouble is to immerse the float in boiling water, when bubbles will reveal the location of any pinholes. Immediately bubbling has ceased, the puncture may be sealed with a trace of solder. This should be considered as a temporary repair only. It is best to fit a new float at the earliest opportunity.

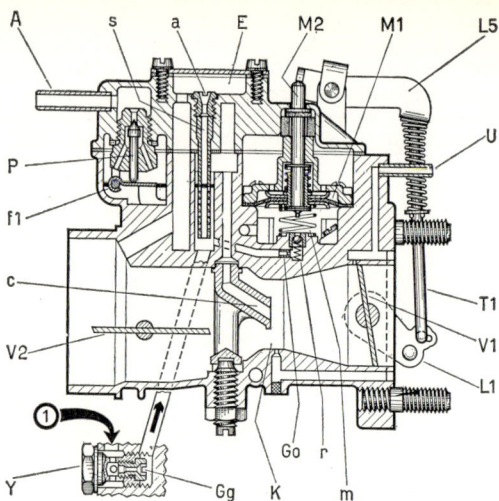

FIG. 31. ANOTHER SECTION THROUGH THE CARBURETTOR FITTED TO
1600A AND EARLY 1500 MODELS, ILLUSTRATING THE
COMPONENTS OF THE ACCELERATION PUMP

Key to Figs. 28–31

A	Connecting tube for fuel pipe	m	Pump diaphragm spring
B	Throttle body	n	Cylinder
C	Body	o	Econostat tube
D	Float chamber cover	P	Needle valve
E	Air space	R	Accelerator pump
a	Air-correction jet	r	Accelerator pump spring
a/s	Air-correction jet with emulsion tube	s	Emulsion tube
c	Spraying nozzle	st1	Bi-metal coil
e	Float-chamber venting tube	T	Pump control rod
F	Float	U	Connecting tube for dual depression
f1	Float lever		take off
Gg	Main jet	U1	Depression piston
Go	Pump jet	U2	Depression channel
g	Slow-running jet	u	Pilot air drilling
H1, 2	Non-return ball valve	V1	Throttle butterfly
i	Injector tube	V2	Strangler butterfly
K	Choke tube	v1	Throttle spindle
L1	Throttle lever	v2	Strangler spindle
L2	Pump intermediate lever	W	Slow-running volume control screw
L3, 5	Pump lever	Y	Main jet carrier
M, M1	Pump diaphragm	1	Fuel passage
M2	Pump rod		

If the engine stops, apparently through lack of fuel, a possible cause is that the float needle has stuck in the closed position. The needle-valve assembly should be unscrewed and cleaned in petrol.

Carburettor Air Cleaner. The mileage at which the air cleaner needs attention will depend, of course, on the conditions under which the car is driven. In dusty conditions it will need more frequent attention, but 5,000 miles is normally the maximum mileage at which the air cleaner should be serviced.

The felt type of filter unit fitted to earlier 1200 engines cannot be dismantled. It should be cleaned by pouring petrol through the intake opening. Allow the felt to dry before refitting it to the engine.

The oil-bath type of air cleaner fitted to single-carburettor engines can be cleaned by removing it from the carburettor, undoing the wing-nut and turning the upper part in the direction of the embossed marks to free it from the base.

On twin-carburettor engines, unclip the connecting rod between the bell-crank and the right-hand carburettor, and also disconnect the electrical cables from the automatic choke and the slow-running jet solenoid, when fitted, and the control wire from the warm-air intake lever, if this is thermostatically controlled. Pull the crankcase breather hose off the intake and loosen the clip on the bellows.

After removing the central wing-nut and slackening the left-hand and right-hand wing-nuts, lift the cleaner off the engine and remove the upper part by loosening the five clips.

Empty the oil and clean out any accumulation of sludge. The filter should be washed in petrol or paraffin (Kerosene) and the air cleaner body filled with fresh engine oil up to the level mark.

Cleaning the Carburettor. A thorough inspection and cleaning of the carburettor is necessary only at fairly long intervals or when carburation trouble is experienced. The preliminary work includes removal of the air cleaner, disconnecting the fuel line between the carburettor and the fuel pump and removing the screws that attach the float chamber cover to the body of the carburettor. The cover can then be lifted and swung backwards. If it is desired to remove it completely, it will be necessary to disconnect the choke cable and the throttle connector link. Normally, however, this is not necessary when it is desired only to clean out the float chamber bowl and jets.

Be careful not to damage the gasket which is fitted between the cover and the body of the carburettor. Any air leakage past the gasket will upset the carburation. The safest plan is to buy a new gasket before dismantling the carburettor, and to fit this on reassembly.

Next, the float toggle lever must be removed so that the float can be lifted out with the aid of a hooked length of thin wire. The float chamber bowl can then be swilled out and any sediment removed with a clean cloth wrapped around the finger.

The float should be carefully examined for any signs of damage and may, as a precaution, be tested by immersing it in hot water. If a leak exists, air and vaporized fuel will be expelled in the form of a stream of small bubbles. As mentioned earlier, it is better to renew a leaky float rather

Fig. 32. The Jets, 1200, 1300 and 1500 Models

1. Slow-running jet   3. Main jet
2. Emulsifying tube   4. Jet carrier

than to attempt to repair it by soldering, since if any appreciable amount of solder is applied, the weight of the float will be upset. A small spot of solder may, however, be applied to cure a pin-hole leak in a metal float.

The float needle-valve is a very important item. If the valve leaks, the fuel level will be too high and excessive consumption may result. It is a simple matter to unscrew the needle-valve and to swill it in petrol. In time, as a result of vibration, the needle-valve and its seating will become ridged and it will not be possible to obtain a perfect seal. It is never advisable to attempt to grind the valve on to its seating; fit a new assembly.

The arrangement of the main, slow-running (or pilot) and air-correction jets is shown in the various illustrations. The main jet and slow-running jet can be removed from outside the carburettor body. The air-correction jet is accessible only after the float chamber cover has been taken off. When a solenoid cut-off valve is fitted, this must be disconnected and unscrewed to remove the slow-running jet.

All the jets and passages in the carburettor body should be blown out with compressed air, preferably using a garage air line, although a tyre pump can be used when no other source of pressure is available. Never be tempted to probe the jets or passages with a piece of wire; the orifices in the jets are drilled to an extreme degree of accuracy and even their internal finish affects the rate of petrol flow. If a jet is found to have been damaged in this way, a replacement of the correct size should be fitted.

When reassembling the carburettor, several points should be borne in mind. Do not forget to fit the washer beneath the float needle-valve. Make sure that the gasket between the float chamber and the float chamber cover is in good condition and is correctly positioned. When the float toggle lever is being refitted, the word "Oben" must be upwards. When the float chamber cover is being re-installed, care should be taken that the tube that projects from the jointing face of the carburettor fits snugly into the cover.

If the choke control cable, on earlier engines, has been disconnected, it should be verified that the choke valve is fully open when the operating knob is pushed in. The choke valve shaft, the throttle valve shaft and the control linkage should be lubricated with engine oil.

When finally fitting the air cleaner, the clamping screw should not be overtightened, as there is a risk of distorting the air horn and thus causing the choke valve to stick. When the carburettor has been reassembled the idling speed and mixture strength should be adjusted as previously described.

THE FUEL INJECTION SYSTEM

As was emphasized at the beginning of this chapter, the fuel-injection system fitted to 411E models should not be tampered with. If misfiring, loss of power or heavy fuel consumption are thought to be attributable to the system, the help of a VW service station should be enlisted. A brief description of the somewhat complicated injection system and its controls may be of interest, however, and will help to explain the reasons behind this advice.

The general layout of the components is shown in Fig. 33. The mechanical side of the system is quite straightforward. Fuel is drawn from the tank by the electrically-operated fuel pump, through a replaceable filter, and is delivered into a pipeline which feeds the four fuel injectors. Before the fuel can return to the tank it must pass through a pressure regulator which maintains a pressure of 28 lb/sq in. (2 kg/sq cm) in the pipes that feed the fuel injectors. Surplus fuel then flows back to the tank through a return pipe which is not under pressure. The overflow from the fuel pump is also fed into this line.

Each injector injects fuel into the inlet pipe—not directly into the combustion chamber—and contains a valve which is operated by an electromagnet, which is in turn triggered by one of a pair of contacts in the ignition distributor. To keep the control unit as simple as possible,

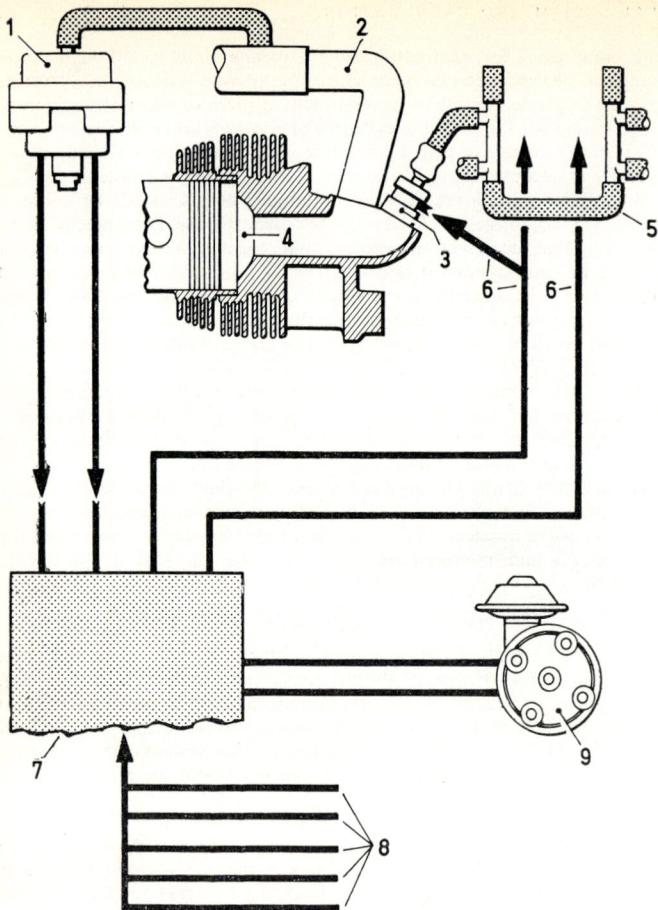

FIG. 33. THE INJECTION AND CONTROL COMPONENTS OF THE FUEL-
INJECTION SYSTEM USED ON 411E MODELS, SHOWN DIAGRAMMATICALLY.

1. Pressure sensor
2. Air-distribution pipe to cylinder
3. Electronically-controlled fuel injector
4. Engine combustion chamber
5. Fuel-supply pipe carrying fuel at constant pressure
6. Control wires from electronic control unit to injectors

7. Electronic injection control unit which computes signals received from sensors
8. Input wires from temperature sensors, pressure switch and throttle-valve switch
9. Ignition distributor, containing speed-sensing trigger contacts

pairs of fuel injectors operate together. Because of this the injectors for cylinders 1 and 3 inject fuel past the open inlet valves during the inlet stoke, but the injectors for cylinders 2 and 4 inject fuel while the inlet valves are still closed. The fact that the fuel is "stored" for a short period in the inlet manifold before the valve opens does not have any adverse effects in practice.

Since the fuel is delivered to the injectors at a constant pressure, the amount that is injected before each firing stroke depends on the time that the injector is open. It is here that the sophisticated electronic control gear comes into the picture. To describe the control system in detail would call for a long chapter, and in the space available it is possible only to give a very brief outline of the general principles.

The time that the injection valves are open is "computed" by the cigar-box-sized electronic control unit, which is mounted in the engine compartment. This receives the necessary information regarding the engine operating conditions from the following sources: the load on the engine is measured by two pressure sensors, and the speed by the rate of opening and closing of the trigger contacts in the ignition distributor; the engine temperature, including cold-starting and warming-up conditions, is measured by temperature sensors in the cylinder head and crankcase; the quantity of fuel needed for full-load conditions is determined by a pressure switch, and the reduced amount needed during deceleration, by a throttle-valve switch and also by the distributor trigger contacts.

The electrical connections from all the units shown in Fig. 33 are fed into the electronic control unit through a wiring harness which is coupled to a 25-pin plug, thus allowing the control unit to be changed quickly when necessary.

The injection system normally requires little or no maintenance, apart from fitting a new fuel filter at 12,000-mile intervals. It is as well, however, to let a VW dealer check the system over at, say, 6,000-mile intervals, in order to forestall possible trouble.

The only adjustment that is within the scope of the average owner is to alter the engine idling speed, if necessary. When the engine is idling the throttle valve is completely closed and the air passes through a small by-pass passage. This is regulated by an adjustable screw in the air distributor which supplies the four inlet pipes, close to the point at which it is connected to the air cleaner.

Unscrewing the adjuster increases the idling speed, and screwing it in decreases the speed. The amount of fuel is regulated automatically.

THE FUEL PUMP

On engine fitted with carburettors, fuel is fed under pressure to the carburettor by a Solex diaphragm-type pump which is bolted to the crankcase and which is operated by an eccentric on the distributor driving shaft. On the earlier type of pump shown in Fig. 34, as the shaft revolves, the

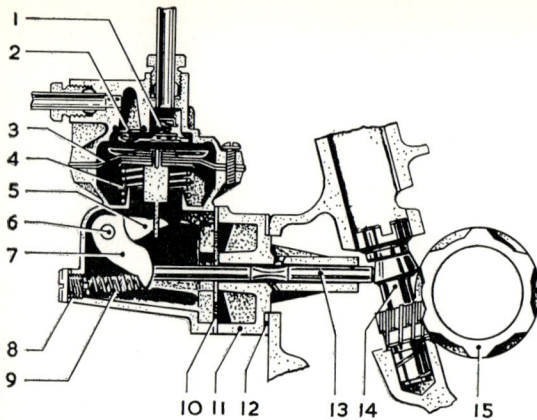

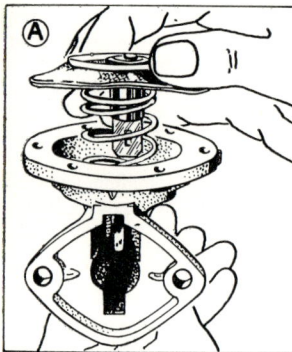

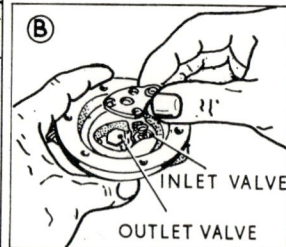

FIG. 34. THE EARLIER FUEL PUMP

1. Outlet valve
2. Inlet valve
3. Diaphragm
4. Diaphragm spring
5. Inner rocker
6. Pivot
7. Outer rocker
8. Drain plug
9. Rocker return spring
10. Gasket
11. Pump extension piece
12. Gasket
13. Push-rod
14. Cam
15. Driving gear

eccentric moves a push-rod outwards. This in turn operates a rocker arm which pulls the diaphragm of the pump downwards against spring pressure, drawing fuel through the inlet valve in the diaphragm chamber. When the rocker arm returns, spring pressure forces the diaphragm upwards and expels the fuel through the outlet valve.

If the carburettor float chamber is full, the needle-valve will be closed by the float and it will not be possible for fuel to enter the float chamber. The pressure of the fuel in the pump chamber will then hold the diaphragm depressed against spring pressure and the flow of fuel will cease, as the rocker arm idles without moving the diaphragm. It will be evident, therefore, that the pressure of the fuel delivered by the pump is determined by the strength of the diaphragm return spring and is not normally influenced by the speed at which the engine is running.

Servicing the Pump. The pump normally requires no service or attention. If symptoms of fuel starvation occur, a VW dealer will be able to fit a special pressure gauge to the outlet of the pump in order to check its operation and, if necessary, will install a reconditioned pump.

Dismantling and reassembling the pump is not a task that should ordinarily be undertaken by the owner. A special gauge is needed to adjust the stroke of the pump and the pressure after reassembly should be checked with the aid of a gauge just referred to. When it is quite impossible to enlist the aid of a VW agent, however, the diaphragm may be renewed or the inlet and outlet valve may be replaced by a practically-minded owner provided that care is taken not to alter the stroke of the operating plunger that projects from the crankcase.

The procedure is first to remove the pump from the engine and then to unscrew the six screws that retain the pump cover to the body. The diaphragm should next be pressed downwards and disconnected from the rocker arm link. The new diaphragm, which is supplied complete with its pull-rod, can then be fitted.

The valves are housed in the pump cover. After the screws securing the valve-retainer plate have been slackened, the plate can be allowed to rise against spring pressure, care being taken not to allow the components to jump out of place. The valve seats should be inspected and the valves should be renewed as a routine precaution.

When placing the valves in position, make sure that their lapped sides are in contact with the valve seats. Notice also that the outlet valve spring must be placed beneath the valve (as viewed with the cover inverted on the bench) while the inlet valve spring is placed on top of the valve disc. With the springs balanced in position and the inlet valve resting on its spring, the valve-retainer plate can be carefully slipped into place and pressed down while the three screws are evenly tightened.

The cover can now be fitted to the pump, but before the retaining screws are tightened down the rocker arm must be pressed inwards to a distance of 1·4 in. (36 mm) in order to flex the diaphragm. Normally, a special gauge is used, but in an emergency it should be possible to cut a short wooden plunger to the required length and to place this in the base chamber of the pump, which can then be gripped between the jaws of the vice so that the plunger presses against the rocker-arm and thus flexes the diaphragm to the correct extent.

The flange screws should then be tightened progressively, working diagonally across the flanges to avoid distortion.

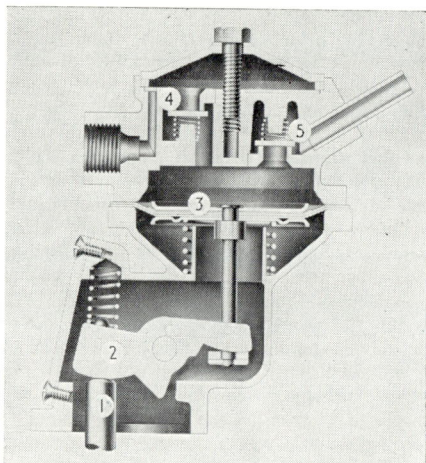

FIG. 35. THE LATER TYPE OF FUEL PUMP

1. Push-rod	4. Inlet valve
2. Rocker arm	5. Outlet valve
3. Diaphragm	

The lower pump chamber should be filled with anti-freezing grease (Universal grease VW–A052) which becomes liquid at operating temperatures. When the pump is fitted to the engine, oil will also reach the linkage through the push-rod bore. If, on removing the pump, the rocker-arms and push-rod are found to be free from grease or oil, a leaking diaphragm is indicated.

The fuel pump fitted to utility vehicle engines from May, 1959, onwards and to cars from August, 1960, works on much the same principle but the diaphragm is drawn down by a vertical push-rod, as can be seen from Fig. 35. On this type of pump a detachable filter cover is fitted to the upper casting. This can be removed by undoing the centre screw, allowing the filter gauze to be withdrawn for cleaning—a job which should normally be necessary only at 6,000-mile intervals.

When the filter has been replaced, make sure that the washer beneath the cover and also that beneath the retaining bolt is in good condition, as an air leak at either point can put the pump completely out of action or cause fuel starvation owing to the presence of air bubbles in the petrol. Otherwise, the servicing of the pump is very similar to that described for the earlier model, the basic differences being evident as the parts are dismantled.

The fuel pump fitted to the 1300 and 1600 models is again basically similar to the design used on earlier engines, but the filter takes the form of a cone which is retained by the petrol-inlet union. To service it, pull the fuel pipe off the inlet, unscrew the union and wash the filter thoroughly in petrol. When the petrol pump is enclosed by a cover, this must, of course, first be removed, after taking off the locking ring.

There is one further point to bear in mind. On the later cars which are not fitted with petrol taps, it will be necessary to shut off the flow of fuel to the pump, either by pinching the flexible pipe or by disconnecting it from the inlet union of the pump and blocking the end with a tapered wooden plug, before removing the filter cover or unscrewing the inlet union to extract the conical type of filter.

FUEL TAP

This tap is fitted only to earlier models. On passenger cars, the tap is turned on when the lever is upwards. When the lever is turned 45° clockwise, the fuel supply is cut off. When the lever is turned 90° clockwise, the reserve supply is available. On utility vehicles, the tap must be pushed in to give the main supply and pulled out for reserve, the intermediate position being "off." On later-model cars on which a fuel gauge is provided, there is no "reserve" position of the fuel tap.

A useful extension for the fuel tap fitted to earlier cars can be made from a length of $\frac{3}{8}$ in. diameter rod, about 20 in. long. One end should be bent through a right-angle and filed with a slight taper so that it is a snug fit in the handle of the tap. A $\frac{1}{8}$ in. hole should be drilled through the handle and extension to take a split-pin, which projects forwards, should be bent into a loop to form a convenient handle.

Normally the fuel tap will give a long period of service without attention. If, however, the tap begins to show signs of leakage, this can be both unpleasant and dangerous if petrol fumes accumulate inside the car. It is a fairly simple matter to renew the rubber seal within the tap but it will first be necessary to drain and remove the fuel tank, before the fuel tap can be unscrewed. The split-pin must be removed from the end of the tap-operating rod. Then, with the right-hand front wheel removed, the operating rod can be withdrawn. The four tank mounting screws can then be unscrewed and the tank lifted out.

After unscrewing the fuel tap, the fuel tank should be flushed out with fuel and blown out with compressed air.

Three different types of fuel tap have been used, but in each case the construction is similar.

In one type the spindle of the tap is retained by a slotted nut which surrounds the spindle. Beneath this nut is a spring and a washer which bears against a flange on the spindle, which in turn rests against the sealing rubber. The stop-pin should be unscrewed from the tap. Next, a slotted screwdriver is needed to unscrew the retaining ring but it should be a fairly simple matter to improvise a tool for this purpose. Dismantling is then quite straightforward and a new seal can be fitted.

On the two alternative designs of tap, the spring, together with a retaining washer, is held in place by a circlip. First, unscrew the stop-pin from the tap as before and then, with a piece of tube, press the spring cap downwards, thus allowing the circlip to be prised out of its groove. The spindle and seal can then be removed. It is always advisable to fit a new circlip when reassembling. It is also important to use only the correct seal as supplied by the VW agent, since other types of rubber are liable to be affected by the fuel.

ADDITIONAL FUEL FILTER

On early models a fuel filter is embodied with the fuel tap. The filter takes the form of a small element retained in a bowl that is secured to the base of a tap by a stirrup. When the knurled nut or wing nut has been slackened, the stirrup can be swung aside and the filter removed. This job is often overlooked since the filter is accessible only from below the car or through an inspection opening in the bodywork, which can be seen when the right-hand front wheel has been removed.

From August 1955 onwards only the filter extending upwards from the fuel tap into the tank is fitted. To clean this filter the tap must be removed as previously described. In this instance, however, the filter is continuously swilled by the surging of fuel in the tank so that attention is not normally required.

When the car is operated mainly on fuel drawn from barrels or cans, as is the case in some overseas territories, the local VW agent can install a fine-filter element in the pipe-line leading from the tank to the fuel pump. As this calls for modification of the pipe and the fitting of suitable unions, the work is best left to an expert. The auxiliary filter, being positioned close to the petrol pump, is easily accessible for routine cleaning.

5 The ignition system

THE ignition system can be responsible for a number of faults—some of which may be difficult to diagnose quickly—if maintenance is neglected. This is borne out by the experience of the road patrols operated by the Royal Automobile Club and the Automobile Association, which has shown that the majority of roadside breakdowns are caused by ignition troubles.

The time spent in keeping the ignition system in first-class condition, therefore, will be more than repaid by enhanced performance, better fuel consumption and trouble-free starting during the winter months.

How the Spark Occurs. The ignition coil, which draws its current from the car battery, contains two windings surrounding an iron core; the primary, a relatively heavy winding, consists of a few hundred turns and is wound over the secondary winding, which is made up of many thousands of turns of fine wire.

When the ignition is switched on and the tungsten contacts in the combined distributor and contact-breaker are closed, current flows from the battery through the primary winding and, through the contact points and the metal of the engine and chassis, back to the battery.

When the contact-breaker points are opened by a rotating four-lobed cam, the current flowing through this primary winding is interrupted and a surge of high-voltage current is set up in the secondary winding.

The surge of high-voltage current, which may amount to twenty thousand volts or more, passes from the central terminal of the ignition coil to the central terminal on the distributor cap. From this point it travels down through a spring-loaded brush or contact to the rotating distributor rotor, which passes in turn each of four electrodes within the distributor cap. Each electrode is connected, in the correct sequence, to a sparking plug (through the sparking plug lead) the firing order of the engine being 1,4,3,2.

When the pulse of current reaches the central electrode of the sparking plug it has no option but to jump across the gap between the central electrode and the side electrode, which is, of course "earthed" through the body of the sparking plug to the metal of the engine. To say that the current has no option but to jump the gap assumes, of course, that both the internal and the external insulators of the sparking plug are clean and in good condition; otherwise the current can leak across one of these insulators to the metal of the plug body without jumping the gap.

Without going into technicalities, it will be seen that the efficiency of the ignition system depends on good connexions at the battery terminals, the low-tension terminals on the coil and distributor, the terminals at the top of the coil and at the centre of the distributor cap, and also on the condition of those vital items, the contact-breaker points within the distributor itself. If these points are burnt or badly pitted the flow of current through them will be insufficient to generate a satisfactory pulse of high-tension current in the secondary windings of the coil. Burnt points may be caused only by age or neglect; but they may also be caused by an inefficient ignition condenser. The method of cleaning and, if necessary, renewing these points, is described later in this chapter.

The Ignition Coil. The ignition coil is the one item in the system which usually requires little attention. Beyond keeping the exterior surface clean and occasionally checking the tightness of the two low-tension terminals, there is little that can be done. The central high-tension terminal should be checked to ensure that it is clamped in the moulded cap of the coil. If any of the wires appears perished it should be renewed; frayed or corroded wiring at the terminals should be cut back and the connexions remade with sound wire. This applies also to any of the high-tension wires between the distributor and the sparking plugs.

THE DISTRIBUTOR

The distributor is driven from the camshaft at half the engine speed. The ignition timing is varied automatically by a centrifugal governor. Because a greater degree of ignition advance is required as engine speed rises, the governor weights are arranged to advance the ignition progressively against the tension of two small springs.

On later cars, a vacuum-operated ignition control supplements the governor weights. This is connected by a pipeline to the carburettor, just on the engine side of the throttle valve, so that it has no effect when the throttle is closed and the engine is idling.

When the throttle is partly closed under cruising conditions, however, a strong depression exists in the induction system of the engine and this is used to advance the ignition beyond the point determined by the centrifugal governor weights, with beneficial effects on fuel consumption. If the throttle is opened, however, the depression in the induction system is reduced and the vacuum-operated control retards the ignition, thus preventing detonation or "pinking" when the engine is under load.

On engines fitted to utility vehicles from May, 1959, and to cars from August, 1960, onwards, the advance and retard of the ignition timing is controlled solely by inlet manifold vacuum, centrifugal timing weights no longer being fitted. Depending on the amount of throttle opening, the vacuum is drawn either from the throttle butterfly position or from the venturi, giving an improved advance curve and greater economy in the lower and medium speed ranges.

On Karmann-Ghia models from January, 1960, onwards, a Bosch distributor having a reference number ZV/PAW 4 R1 or ZV/PAUR 4 R1 is fitted. The latter has a rotor which eliminates radio and television interference, whereas the other type of distributor does not have this refinement.

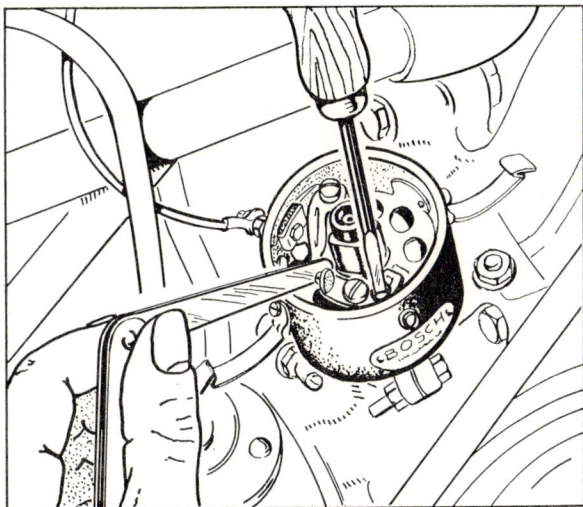

FIG. 36. ADJUSTING DISTRIBUTOR CONTACT-BREAKER POINTS

From February, 1960, onwards, special plug leads which incorporate radio and T.V. suppressors are fitted. These leads, which can be identified by their red colour, should not be cut but should be renewed in sets.

Servicing the Distributor. When the two spring clips on either side of the distributor have been released, the cap, complete with ignition cables, may be lifted off, revealing the rotor arm and contact-breaker mechanism.

Carefully wipe the inside and outside of the cap, paying particular attention to the spaces between the leads and terminals. Check that the small carbon brush in the centre of the cap works freely in its holder, but be careful not to break it.

The contact point operated by the cam should be moved away from the fixed point with a finger to the allow two points to be examined. They should have a clean, grey frosted appearance. The formation of a slight "pip" on one point and a corresponding crater on the other is quite normal after several thousand miles of running.

If the points are oily, they should be cleaned with a rag moistened with petrol but if badly pitted or blackened they must be lightly dressed flat and parallel with a fine file or a fine-grade carborundum stone. The contact-breaker lever carrying the movable point should be removed to allow the points to be cleaned or trued-up. This can be done, on later distributors, by disconnecting the cable from the low-tension terminal on the side of the distributor, loosening the nut on the terminal screw and taking off the contact-breaker arm cable. The spring clip and washer should be removed from the contact-breaker arm pivot and the spring and insulator disconnected from the terminal on the base-plate. The arm can then be removed.

The fixed point is renewed by taking out the locking screw and removing the screw that passes through the push-rod bracket.

On earlier distributors the job is equally straightforward. The only point to watch, in each case, is the position of the insulating washers.

Badly-pitted or burnt contact points should be renewed; no amount of truing-up will make them serviceable. As replacement contacts must be fitted only as a pair it is necessary to remove the fixed contact as just described.

It is a sound plan to fit new contact-breaker points and also a new condenser, whenever a new set of plugs is installed at 10,000 mile intervals. The extra cost will be well repaid by improved performance, better petrol consumption and easier starting. The contact-breaker points are the heart of the engine.

When reassembling the distributor a thin smear of petroleum jelly should be applied to the cam and a small drop of oil placed on the pivot pin before the movable contact point is fitted.

Test the freedom of the advance and retard weights by replacing the rotor and attempting to turn it in either direction by hand. It should turn slightly in a clockwise direction and spring back to the static position.

Adjusting the Contact-breaker Gap. The contact-breaker points should be set when the fibre arm of the moving contact is on the highest point of the cam. Remove the sparking plugs and turn the engine with a spanner applied to the generator pulley nut. Check the gap by sliding the feeler gauge squarely between the points. If a pip and crater have formed, it will be impossible to obtain a true reading. The points should, therefore, be renewed or refaced as just described. There should be just a slight drag. If the gap is too small or too wide, adjustment is necessary; this is done by slackening the adjustment lock screws on the fixed contact plate and moving the plate until there is a gap of 0·016 in. (0·4 mm) between the points.

After setting the gap, tighten the lock screws and make another check, as it is possible slightly to alter the gap while tightening-up the screws. The ignition timing must then be checked, since an alteration of 0·004 in. (0·1mm) in the distributor gap will change the timing by 3 degrees of crankshaft rotation.

Ignition Timing. Let us first consider the case in which the distributor has been removed from the 1200 engine. The crankshaft should be rotated until the notch on the fan belt pulley lines up with the joint between the two halves of the crankcase just to the right of the distributor. The slot in the distributor driving shaft should be nearly parallel with the fan pulley and towards the rear of the engine—that is, towards the operator.

On utility vehicle engines from May, 1959, onwards and on car engines from August, 1960, if the crankshaft pulley has only one timing mark, this indicates 7·5° b.t.d.c. When 10° of advance is specified (see data tables in Chapter 9) it will be necessary to file another notch in the pulley, 4 mm to the right of the original notch, as viewed from above. When two notches are already provided, the left-hand one indicates 7·5° b.t.d.c. and the right-hand notch, 10° b.t.d.c.

If it is essential to use low-grade petrol and if pinking is experienced, the engine should be timed to 7·5° b.t.d.c.

The distributor spindle should be rotated until the rotor arm points to the line across the rim of the distributor body, corresponding to the position of No. 1 sparking plug electrode in the cap. The distributor can now be slid into place, slightly rotating the rotor in either direction until the offset driving dogs engage.

Slacken the clamping-plate pinch-bolt and rotate the distributor body so that the vacuum-control unit (if fitted) is towards the rear and turned at an angle of about 45° to the centre-line of the engine. In this position the contact-breaker points should be just opening if they have been set to the correct gap.

Turn the distributor clockwise until the points are definitely closed and then rotate it very gently anti-clockwise until the points just begin to separate. If the ignition is switched on, a spark can be heard to jump the points at this instant. Tighten the clamp bolt without disturbing the setting.

The procedure is similar with the 1300 engine, except that the left-hand notch on the pulley should be lined up with the crankcase joint. On the 1500 and 1600 models, the notches in the pulley are visible through an opening in the sheet-metal housing which encloses the pulley and must be aligned with the projection on the fan housing which lines-up with the inspection opening. The correct timing is as follows:

1500 models: Right-hand notch aligned with indicator on fan housing.

1500S models: Centre notch aligned with indicator.

1600 models: Left-hand notch aligned with indicator.

In the case of 411 and 411E models, the initial timing of 5° b.t.d.c. is set by aligning the black mark on the fan with the indicator. This is only a provisional setting, and the red mark should be aligned with the indicator, with the engine running at 3,500 r.p.m., by using a stroboscope, to give a timing of 27° b.t.d.c. As this adjustment calls for the use of a stroboscopic timing lamp and a tachometer, the check will normally have to be left to a VW dealer.

Checking the Static Ignition Timing. In order to check the precise moment at which the points break contact, a 6-watt bulb mounted in a suitable holder may be connected across the two low-tension terminals at the top of the ignition coil. The ignition should be switched on and the engine rotated. When the points are closed the lamp will light up; at the instant they open it will be extinguished. It is a simple matter, therefore, to set the engine to top-dead-centre as just described, slacken the distributor clamp, turn the distributor clockwise until the lamp lights up, and then anti-clockwise until it is just extinguished.

If the distributor has not been removed from the engine it will, of course, be sufficient to carry out only the timing test and to slacken the distributor clamp to allow a slight readjustment to be made if necessary.

THE SPARKING PLUGS

Difficult starting or misfiring can be caused by dirty sparking plugs or incorrect plug gaps. It is important, therefore, that both the inside and outside of the sparking plugs should receive regular attention. The portion of the insulator projecting above the body of the sparking plug should be kept clean by wiping it with a dry, clean rag. An oily insulator provides a "track" to earth. If difficulty is experienced in starting, therefore, particularly in winter months, do not continue to operate the starter. First wipe the sparking plug insulators, caps and rubber leads. Unless other ignition faults are present the engine should then start readily.

Prolonged use of the starter causes conditions to become worse instead of better: first, the sparking plug internal insulators become wet with petrol, preventing a spark occurring at the plug points. This will necessitate the removal and drying of the plugs—an operation which may have to be carried out more than once because of the large amount of petrol present in the combustion chambers.

Secondly, if the battery is in a low state of charge the voltage will be further reduced and may be insufficient for the ignition circuit during the period when the starter motor is operating.

Cleaning and Inspecting Sparking Plugs. On the 1500S and 1600 models it will be necessary to remove the air cleaner before unscrewing the plugs. It is also advisable to unhook the return springs from the carburettor pull-rods. The plug spanner must be handled carefully to avoid cracking the insulator. Make sure, before applying any force to the tommy-bar.

DIAGNOSING SPARKING PLUG TROUBLES

PLUG CONDITION	POSSIBLE CAUSE	REMEDY
Insulator: Clean, coloured straw to coffee *Body*: Light carbon deposit	Plug condition: correct	
Insulator: Fluffy grey or yellowish deposit *Body*: Fluffy or yellowish grey deposit	Plug condition: correct Deposit due to premium petrol	
Insulator: Clean, coloured straw to coffee *Body*: Hard carbon deposits	Too much oil reaching plugs Unsuitable oil Too much upper cylinder lubricant	Clean and reset plugs Check piston rings and valve guides Drain and refill with correct grade Reduce upper cylinder lubricant
Insulator: Clean, white or pale *Electrodes*: Partly worn (after short service) *Body*: Clean	Plug too *hot* Carburettor mixture too weak Ignition too far advanced	Fit *cooler* plug Adjust carburettor for richer mixture Retard spark
Insulator: Sooted-up *Body*: Sooty	Mixture too rich Ignition too far retarded Plug too *cool*	Check for excessive use of choke Adjust carburettor for weaker mixture Advance spark Fit *hotter* plug
Insulator: Sooted and oiled-up *Body*: Sooted and oiled-up	plug too *cool* Mixture too rich Too much oil	Fit *hotter* plug Adjust carburettor for weaker mixture Check piston rings and valve guides Check for too much oil in sump Reduce upper cylinder lubricant
Insulator: Cracked inside	Damaged during electrode adjustment Plug too *hot* Mixture too weak	Fit new plug, adjust gap by bending side electrode *only* Fit *cooler* plug Adjust carburettor for richer mixture
Insulator: Dark, blistered, cracked or partly glazed	Plug too *hot* for premium petrol	Fit *cooler* plug for use with premium petrol

that the spanner fits securely over the plug. After unscrewing the plugs see that the sealing washers do not fall off and become lost.

As modern plugs cannot be dismantled for cleaning, the carbon deposits must be removed by the use of a plug-cleaning machine in which a high-pressure air blast carries a fine abrasive into the interior of the plug, effectively scouring the insulator, the inner walls and points.

Adjusting Sparking Plug Gaps. Throughout its working life the sparking plug is subjected to very high temperatures. Inevitably, after some

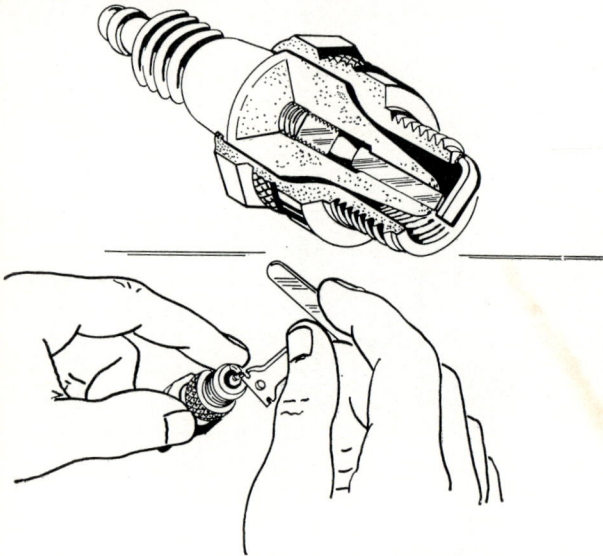

FIG. 37. SPARKING PLUG, SHOWN PARTLY SECTIONED, AND THE METHOD OF ADJUSTING THE SIDE ELECTRODE WITH A SPECIAL GAUGE TOOL

thousands of miles of use, the gap between the electrodes will have widened. It should, therefore, be checked and adjusted at regular intervals. Check the gap with the sparking plug gauge and make any adjustment that may be necessary by bending the side electrode. Most gap-setting tools are specially shaped for this purpose. Otherwise, the side electrode may be tapped towards the centre one either on the bench or with a suitable tool. If the gap is closed too much, do not use the centre electrode as a support when levering the side electrode up; this may crack the insulator.

The feeler blade should just slide between the electrodes when the gap is set at 0·028 in., (0·7 mm) which is the gap that will give the best results for most types of plug. If a gauge of the correct thickness is not available, a normal combination-set of mechanic's feelers should be used, the required thickness being made by using two or more blades together.

The threaded portions of the plugs should be cleaned with a stiff wire brush and a smear of graphite grease placed on the threads. This will ensure that the plugs will tighten down easily and facilitate removal when the next cleaning and adjustment is due. Make sure that the sealing washers are in good condition and tighten the plugs, using hand pressure only on the tommy-bar to ensure a gas-tight joint. Too much force should never be used and is unnecessary.

Sparking Plugs as a Guide to Engine Condition. Irregularities in carburation, distribution and so on can usually be detected by examining the internal insulators of the sparking plugs after the engine has been switched off while running at a reasonably high speed. This avoids the clouding effect produced by the idling mixture, which is richer than the normal mixture.

The chart on page 83 (drawn up by the manufacturers of A.C. sparking plugs) indicates the symptoms that may be found and the appropriate remedies.

6 Electrical system and auxiliaries

OF all the causes of difficult starting, particularly during cold weather, the battery is often a major culprit. The owner who values his comfort and peace of mind—or simply appreciates efficiency for its own sake!—should remember three golden rules: always keep the battery clean externally and well topped-up; make sure that it is kept charged but not over-charged; and, when the time comes to replace it, buy a first-class battery which incorporates the maximum number of plates per cell and which is built from good materials.

Plain Facts About Your Battery. Many owners are taken aback when confronted by one or two blunt truths concerning their battery. Did you know, for example, that it takes up to 250 amperes to start your engine from cold—and this from a battery which has a capacity of only 66 or 70 ampere-hours at the 20-hour discharge rate (depending on the type fitted)? This means that a current of about $3\frac{1}{2}$ amperes (equivalent to little more than the current used by the side, tail and number-plate lamps, or half the current consumed by one headlamp bulb) can be drawn from a fully-charged battery, in perfect condition, for 20 hours. It also means that the factor of safety of the battery is lower than that of any other component on the car. There may be only enough current stored in the battery to turn a cold engine for less than thirty seconds.

Similarly, lights left burning continuously will run the battery down to less than half-charge in a few hours; and a half-charged battery has not enough energy to turn the starter quickly to ensure a ready start in freezing weather. Another unpleasant fact is that the average battery will have completely exhausted itself within six to eight weeks, due to internal discharge, if it is left uncharged.

On the other hand, the voltage of a 6-volt battery increases to $7\frac{3}{4}$–8 volts during the last stages of charging. Obviously this peak voltage that is obtainable from a fully-charged battery can make an immense difference to starting and can compensate for some voltage-drop caused by pitted contact-breaker points or doubtful connexions in the battery cables, ignition switch or the low-tension circuit—surely a good argument for the use of a trickle charger.

A further argument in favour of regular home-charging is the fact that the relatively short life obtained from many modern batteries can by ascribed to the heavy "boost" charge of 20–30 amperes which the battere receives when the car is driven away after a cold start. The correct normal charging rate for the battery is 5 amperes. The voltage-controller that regulates the output from the generator, however, is specifically designed to give a temporary boosting charge at from five to six times this figure to bring the battery back to a charged condition as quickly as possible. The charging rate then falls to a more normal figure, finally being reduced to a trickle charge as the battery becomes fully charged.

Obviously, if a home trickle charger is installed in the garage and the battery is kept at or near the fully-charged condition, it will have a much easier life, and the cost of the trickle charger will eventually be more than saved; moreover, one has on the credit side the peace of mind that results from the certainty of an immediate start even on the coldest mornings.

Battery Service. On cars the battery is fitted under the rear seat, except for the 411 range, on which the battery is located under the left-hand front seat. On utility vehicles and on the Karmann-Ghia it is in the engine compartment and will therefore need more frequent topping-up, as the heat of the engine causes more rapid evaporation of the electrolyte in the cells. The vent plugs should be kept clean and tight to prevent acid leakage and the battery and the surrounding parts, particularly the top of the cells, clean and dry. If acid is spilled, wipe it away with a clean wet cloth and then dry the part thoroughly; household ammonia will neutralize the acid. The terminals and connexions should be kept free from corrosion and should be smeared with a coating of petroleum jelly.

The level of the electrolyte in the cells of the battery should not be allowed to fall below the tops of the separators; every 1,000 miles (1,600 km.) a check should be made to ensure that the level is $\frac{1}{4}$ in. to $\frac{3}{8}$ in. (6–9 mm.) above the separators. Distilled water only should be added until this level is reached in each cell. It is best to add water just before the cells are to be charged. In cold weather this will allow the acid and water to mix thoroughly and thus avoid any risk of the water freezing and damaging the plates and battery case. It should not be necessary to add acid unless some of the electrolyte has been spilt. If acid is added in order to raise the specific gravity of the electrolyte, the plates may be damaged.

The need for excessive topping-up of all the cells is usually an indication of an unduly high generator charging rate; while if one cell regularly requires more water than the others, a leak in that cell must be suspected. Even a slow leak may, in time, completely drain the acid from a cell. A leaky container should, of course, be replaced immediately, and all parts that have been exposed to the acid should be well swabbed with household ammonia to prevent corrosion.

Specific Gravity of the Electrolyte. The best indication of the state of charge of the cells is the specific gravity of the electrolyte, which can be ascertained by using a hydrometer. A reading should not be taken immediately after adding distilled water, however; the battery should be charged for at least an hour to ensure that the water and acid are thoroughly mixed.

The readings for each of the cells should be approximately the same. A battery in a low state of charge may be recharged by making a long run in daylight or by charging from a d.c. supply at a rate of 5 amperes until the cells are "gassing" freely.

The electrolyte drawn into the hydrometer should be fairly clear; if it is dirty it is probable that the plates are in a bad condition, in which case a VW agent or battery specialist should be consulted.

The specific gravity of the acid in the cells when fully charged should be within 0·005 (5 points) above or 0·010 (10 points) below the values given in the table below.

The specific gravity of the electrolyte varies with the temperature. For convenience in comparing specific gravities this is always corrected to 60°F, which is adopted as a reference temperature. The method of correction is as follows—

For every 5°F *below* 60°F, *deduct* 0·002 from the observed reading to obtain the true specific gravity at 60°F. For every 5°F *above* 60°F *add* 0·002 to the observed reading.

The temperature must be that actually indicated by a thermometer immersed in the electrolyte and not the atmospheric temperature.

SPECIFIC GRAVITY OF ELECTROLYTE
(CORRECTED TO 60°F)

TEMPERATE CLIMATES Normally below 80°F (27°C)		SUB-TROPICAL CLIMATES 80°–100°F (27°–38°C)		TROPICAL CLIMATES Over 100°F (38°C)	
Filling	Fully charged	Filling	Fully charged	Filling	Fully charged
1·350	1·280–1·300	1·320	1·250–1·270	1·300	1·220–1·240

Specific Gravity too Low. At 60°F a half-discharged battery will give readings of about 1·210 per cell while the specific gravity of a discharged cell will fall to below 1·150. If the specific gravity after a prolonged charge is persistently less than the "fully charged" values, it is possible that it may be necessary to add acid to bring the specific gravity up to the correct figure. Whenever possible, however, expert advice should be sought on this point.

Low Specific Gravity on One Cell. This fault (especially if successive readings show the difference to be increasing) indicates that the cell is in poor condition. If the specific gravity is 0·0050 to 0·0075 below that in the other cells and there is no leakage of electrolyte, a partial short-circuit or other trouble within the cell is indicated and a new battery may be required. From experience, an Exide can be recommended.

Idle Batteries. A battery which is to stand idle should be charged at the normal charging rate until the specific gravity is within 0·010 of the fully-charged value. Disconnect the wires from the battery to avoid loss of charge through any small leak in the wiring.

A battery not in active service may be kept in condition for immediate use by giving it a freshening charge at least once every two months. It should, preferably, also be given a thorough charge after an idle period, before it is put into service. It is unwise to allow a battery that is in good condition to stand for more than two months without charging it.

THE DYNAMO OR GENERATOR

A generator of the two-brush voltage-controlled type is fitted to all models except the 411, 411L, 411E and 411LE, which have alternators instead of conventional dynamos—see page 90. The charging rate is automatically controlled by a regulator unit housed, with the cut-out, in the control box. It depends entirely on the state of charge of the battery and is not under the control of the driver.

As has been previously mentioned, *the regulator* automatically provides a large charging current when the battery is discharged so that it is brought back to a fully-charged state in the shortest possible time; on the other hand, a low "trickle" charge is provided for a fully-charged battery in order to keep it in good condition, without the possibility of damage or excessive "gassing" due to persistent overcharging of a charged battery.

The cut-out is a form of automatic switch which disconnects the battery dynamo circuit whenever the engine is stopped or is running at low speeds.

Charge Indicator. The ignition warning lamp acts also as a charge indicator; when it glows it shows that current is flowing in the ignition circuit and that the battery is being discharged by the current taken by the ignition coil (when the contact points are closed) and by any accessories that are controlled by the ignition switch and that are in use at the time. The warning light should be extinguished when the engine is speeded up above the idling speed; if it continues to glow, the dynamo, regulator and cut-out must be tested by an experienced electrician to determine which is faulty.

A low charging rate can usually be traced to a dirty or pitted dynamo commutator or to chipped, worn or binding carbon brushes. At fairly long intervals (say, every 5,000 miles), therefore, remove the dust cover from the dynamo, carefully raise the brush springs with a hooked wire and extract the brushes. Clean out the brush holders with a cloth dipped in petrol. Next clean the commutator by pressing a petrol-damped cloth against it while rotating it by the pulley, after slackening the belt drive. If the commutator is slightly burnt, it can be burnished by using a strip of fine glass-paper folded around a flat piece of wood. Press the glass-paper on the commutator while the engine is idling. Emery cloth should never be used to clean the commutator. If the commutator is badly pitted or scored the dynamo should be returned to the agents for attention.

When replacing the brushes make sure that they are free to move in their holders and bed down properly on the commutator; also check that the brush springs have not lost their tension. The spring tension should not be increased unnecessarily, however, as this will simply cause rapid wear of the brushes.

If the brushes are found to be tight or sticking after the holders have been cleaned, their width may be slightly reduced by rubbing them down on a sheet of glass-paper laid on a flat surface such as a sheet of plate glass.

If the brushes are badly worn or cracked, remove the screws securing the eyelets on the ends of the brush leads. Fit the new brushes into their holders and secure the eyelets on the end of the brush leads in the original position. New brushes are pre-formed to the commutator surface and do not require further bedding down.

The Control Box. The cut-out and regulator are carefully set before they leave the manufacturer's works and should not be tampered with. If the dynamo output does not fall when the battery is fully charged, or the battery becomes abnormally discharged, it will, however, be necessary to call in expert assistance.

The owner should never attempt to carry out adjustments as the use of an accurately calibrated moving-coil voltmeter is essential in order to obtain the correct settings.

Alternator Maintenance. Apart from adjusting the tension of the driving belt and keeping the exterior of the alternator reasonably clean and the terminals tight, this type of generator requires no routine maintenance. If trouble should develop, rectification is definitely a job for a VW dealer or an auto-electrical specialist.

Important points to remember are that the battery should never be disconnected while the alternator is running, nor should the alternator be run with the main output cable disconnected; otherwise the control unit or the alternator diode may be damaged. A garage must take special precautions before using a fast-charger or battery booster, or when carrying out electrical welding on any part of the car.

Fuses. On earlier saloon and convertible models, fuses are fitted in holders in the front luggage compartment, next to the fuel tank, and also at the back of the instrument panel. On later cars and on the Transporter, the fuses are fitted only under the instrument panel or under the tray beneath the panel.

On the 411, 411L, 411E and 411LE there is a separate 8-amp fuse for the heater booster relay which is fitted on the left-hand side of the engine compartment, in a bayonet-action plastic holder. On all 411 models fitted with manual transmissions there is a further 8-amp fuse in a similar holder in the engine compartment, next to the ignition distributor. This fuse protects the reversing lights.

Volkswagen models are generously provided with fuses, so that if a short-circuit occurs in a component or in the wiring serving it, only the appropriate fuse "blows" and the remaining circuits are not put out of action. It is a simple matter to identify the faulty fuse by the blackened appearance of the glass and the melted ends which are visible in the tube, but before fitting a new fuse the fault which caused it to blow must be discovered; otherwise the replacement will fail immediately the defective circuit is switched on.

Carefully check the wiring for signs of chafing or perished or damaged insulation, and the terminals or contacts of the units served by the fuse, for evidence of a short-circuit.

If no faults are found and the new fuse burns out again almost immediately, do not replace it with one which will carry a heavier current, or bridge the clips with wire, since this may overload the circuit and result in serious damage or may even cause a fire. A useful test is to connect a bulb-holder, fitted with a 6-volt, 3-watt bulb, across the fuse clips. Switch

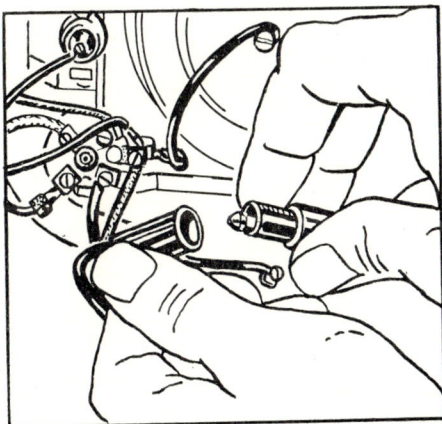

FIG. 38. RENEWING THE FUSE IN A HOLDER CONNECTED INTO THE WIRING BEHIND THE DASHBOARD ON EARLY MODELS

on, in turn, the circuits served by the "blown" fuse and move the wires about to attempt to repeat the fault. When the circuit is switched on, the test lamp may glow faintly but when the trouble occurs, the bulb will light up or flash momentarily with full brilliance.

Engine Earthing Strap. Starting troubles and misfiring can sometimes be traced to a broken earthing wire, fitted between the gearbox and the chassis. An improved braided type of wire, which is quite inexpensive and can be obtained from a VW agent, should eliminate this trouble.

THE STARTER MOTOR

In very cold weather it may be an advantage to depress the clutch pedal to eliminate the drag of the lubricant in the gearbox and prevent unnecessary strain on the starter motor and battery. On the other hand, the friction of the clutch release bearing may slow down the cranking speed. It is advisable to make a test under both conditions. Operate the starter switch firmly and release it immediately the engine fires.

Starter Service. If the starter is sluggish in action, it should be removed from the engine and the commutator and brushes cleaned, preferably by an expert. Assuming that the battery is in a charged condition, the starter should rotate the engine smartly when the switch is operated. The headlamps should be switched on during the test. If the lights go dim, although the starter does not operate, the indication is that the battery is discharged or that current is flowing through the windings of the starter but for some reason the armature is not rotating, possibly due to the starter pinion being already engaged with the flywheel starter-ring.

Should the lamps remain bright, however, the starter switch may be inoperative and should be checked but first make sure that the terminals on the switch are clean and tight.

Freeing a Jammed Starter Pinion. If the starter pinion should become jammed in mesh with the starter ring it can usually be freed by engaging top gear and attempting to push the car forward. Do not engage a lower gear and rock the car violently backwards and forwards: this may jam the pinion more firmly in mesh and may damage the drive. The major effort should be in a forward direction.

If the starter pinion does not engage with the flywheel, the starter drive probably requires cleaning. It will be necessary to unbolt the starter from the engine. The pinion should move freely on the screwed sleeve; if there is any dirt on the sleeve it must be washed off with paraffin. A trace of light machine oil should then be applied to the sleeve; engine oil must not be used owing to the risk of grit accumulating on the sleeve and causing the pinion to stick. If the battery is discharged or weak, the starter may spin once or twice without engaging: this is a useful pointer to a source of trouble that may result in one being stranded until a new battery or a tow can be obtained.

The pre-engaged starter fitted to later models is a rather more complex affair and servicing of the motor and drive is best left to an expert.

THE HEADLAMPS

The headlamps may have separate reflectors and bulbs, or the lamp filaments and reflector may form a "sealed-beam" unit, which must be replaced if a filament should fail. In order to replace a separate head-lamp bulb, on all models except the 411 range loosen the retaining screw at the bottom of a headlamp rim and lift out the lens and reflector unit. The bulb holder can then be removed from the reflector by turning the cap to the left. Pull the connector off the base of the bulb and fit the new bulb, holding it with a clean cloth or with a sheet of paper in order to prevent finger marks which would be burnt on to the glass by the heat of the filament. If a bulb is handled with the bare fingers, wipe it with methylated spirits before fitting it to the headlamp. The lug in the lamp holder must engage with the notch in the reflector and the cap should be inserted so that the contact strip is located on the base of the parking-light bulb.

When a sealed-beam unit is fitted, it can be removed by loosening the screw below the centre of the headlight rim and taking out the complete unit. Pull off the cable connector and disconnect the two cables from the parking bulb holder, when this is fitted. If the sealed-beam unit is retained by five springs, hold it in one hand and ease the springs out with the thumb of the other hand. If the springs are prised out with a screwdriver one may jump out and be lost.

On the 411, 411L, 411E and 411LE the headlamp bulbs can be replaced by opening the front luggage compartment lid, removing a knurled screw and taking the plastic cap off the appropriate headlamp assembly. The bulbs can then be taken out by pulling the cables off the connectors, pulling off the rubber sleeve and unhooking the spring-wire bulb-retaining clip.

Halogen headlamp bulbs should never be touched with the bare fingers. Any finger-marks left on the glass will evaporate, due to the heat which is developed when the bulb is switched on, and the vapour will settle on the reflector and spoil the mirror finish. When inserting a new bulb, make a note of the recess in the reflector which locates it and be careful not to interchange the cables. The brown earthing cable must be fitted to the tab on the side of the reflector and the grey cable for the parking light goes to the lower tab.

Aligning the Headlamps. To obtain the best illumination and to avoid dazzling other motorists when the beams are dipped, it is essential to align the headlamps correctly. This is done by rotating the horizontal and vertical trimming screws which project through the plated rim of the lamp on all models except the 1600, on which it is necessary to remove the plated rim in order to adjust the screws and the 411 models, on which the adjusters are in the form of knurled knobs in the headlamp shroud, which are accessible from inside the front luggage compartment, after taking off the protective caps. Turning the upper screw or the left-hand knob tilts the beam upwards or downwards while the second screw, at the side of the reflector, or the right-hand knob swings the beam in a horizontal plane.

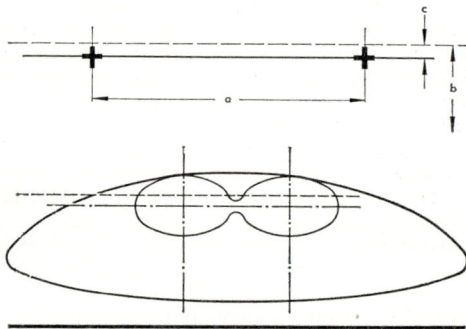

FIG. 39. TYPICAL HEADLAMP ALIGNMENT DIAGRAM

The lower sketch shows how the beams should be lined-up with the marks on the wall (*see* text)

a, distance between headlamp centres. *b*, height of centres above ground. *c*, 2 in. downward deflection.

Most garages today have beam-setting equipment which enables the lamps to be quickly and accurately aligned. Only if it is impossible to make use of this equipment should an attempt be made to readjust the headlamps by trial-and-error methods. Adjust each headlight in turn while the other is covered up. The lamps are correctly aimed if, when switched to main beam, the beams are slightly below horizontal, pointing straight ahead and parallel to one another. The tyres must be inflated to the correct pressures and the driver should be sitting in the driving seat.

VW instruction books give diagrams which may be helpful in setting the lamps, but these presuppose that it is possible to stand the car on an *absolutely level* surface at a distance of 16 ft 6 in. (5 m) or 25 ft (7·5 m) from a vertical wall (depending on whether separate headlamp bulbs or sealed-beam units are fitted) and that accurate aiming points can be drawn on the wall. In practice such diagrams are seldom very useful, as it is difficult to meet all the requirements, but if you do use one, *make sure that it is correct for the side of the road on which the car will be driven.*

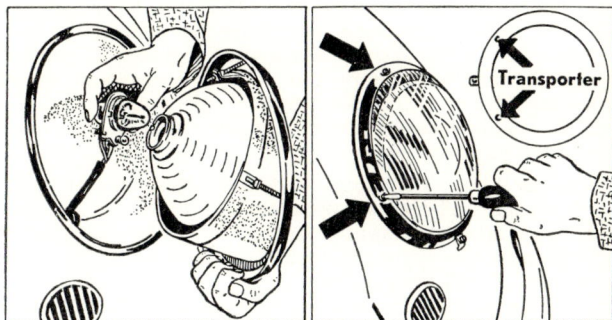

FIG. 40. RENEWING A HEADLAMP BULB AND (*Right*) THE HORIZONTAL AND VERTICAL ADJUSTING SCREWS

Otherwise it is possible to adjust the lamps incorrectly, so that they seriously dazzle oncoming traffic.

INSTRUMENTS AND ACCESSORIES

Speedometer. The speedometer head normally requires no service and as special equipment is required for most repair work it is advisable to send the head to the makers or authorized speedometer service station for overhaul.

If the speedometer cable becomes noisy in operation, however, or the speedometer needle wavers or jerks, the trouble will usually be that the driving cable requires lubrication, preferably with a graphited grease.

The speedometer cable is driven from the left-hand front wheel. In order to withdraw the inner cable it is necessary to unscrew the knurled nut that retains the outer cable at the rear of the speedometer. Next, the nave plate should be removed from the left-hand front wheel and the cotter pin withdrawn from the squared end of the inner cable that projects through the hub cap.

This will allow the outer cable to be withdrawn from the guide sleeve in the stub axle. The inner driving cable can then be drawn out of the outer sleeve. After thoroughly lubricating the cable with graphited grease it can be reassembled in its outer sleeve and connected at each end, making sure that the square at the upper end fits correctly into the recess in the speedometer. If this treatment does not restore a steady speedometer reading, the inner cable probably requires renewal. First, however, inspect the run of the outer cable and correct any sharp bends. Make sure, too, that the cable is not kinked when the front wheels are turned from lock to lock.

One further important service point to check is the condition of the small rubber sealing sleeve that is fitted behind the guide tube in the stub axle. This sleeve is intended to prevent water entering the speedometer cable and the front wheel bearing; if water finds its way in, the wheel bearings are liable to be corroded and the speedometer cable may freeze in winter. The most suitable lubricant at this point is a water-repellent and anti-freezing grease.

Windscreen Wiper. The electric windscreen wiper motor and gearbox is mounted under the bonnet and operates the blades through a linkage.

If the wiper motor develops a fault, it is best to take advantage of the exchange scheme whereby the faulty unit can be exchanged for a reconditioned one at a very moderate cost.

The windscreen washer reservoir fitted to models from August, 1961, onwards has a tyre valve which allows pressure to be built up with a tyre pump or garage inflator, thus feeding the fluid to the jets when the dashboard control is operated. The pressure in the reservoir should, therefore, be topped-up from time to time, and, of course, whenever the reservoir is refilled, to ensure an adequate spray from the jets. The correct pressure is 35 lb per sq in. (2·5 kg/sq. cm) It is usually more convenient to refill the container at a service station, where an air line can be borrowed to pressurize it.

Direction Indicators. Several different makes of indicator have been fitted, the design of which differs slightly in each case, but the method of replacing the bulb in the indicator arm can be discovered on inspection. In all cases the arms may be pulled out and held in the horizontal position without taking any special precautions.

The flashing direction indicators fitted to some models are operated by a flasher unit which opens and closes the circuit automatically. These units require no service and if a fault develops a replacement should be fitted.

7 The brakes

HYDRAULIC brakes are fitted to all except the early standard models, which have mechanically-operated brakes. The handbrake, however, which operates on the rear wheels only, is operated mechanically on all models and thus provides a second line of defence in the unlikely event of the hydraulic system failing.

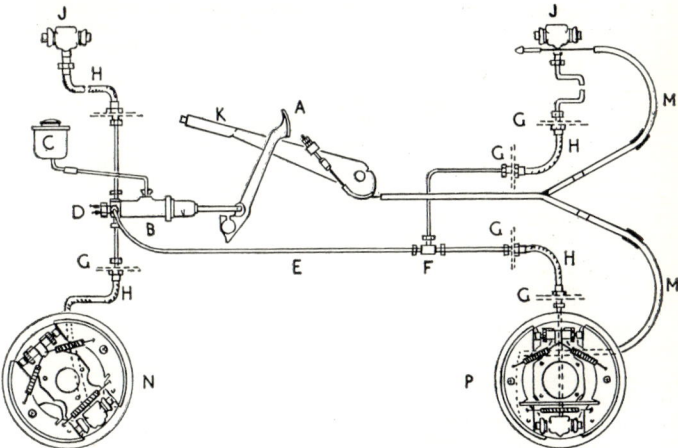

FIG. 41. LAYOUT OF THE EARLIER HYDRAULIC BRAKING SYSTEM

A. Brake pedal	G. Hose bracket
B. Master cylinder	H. Brake hose
C. Fluid reservoir	J. Wheel cylinder
D. Stop light switch	K. Handbrake lever
E. Hydraulic line	M. Cable conduit tube
F. Three-way connexion	N. Front wheel brake

P. Rear wheel brake

Hydraulic Brakes. The hydraulic system comprises a master cylinder in which the hydraulic pressure is originated, a cylinder or cylinders operating the brake shoes on each brake drum, a reservoir from which the brake fluid in the system is replenished, and the pipelines connecting the master cylinder to the wheel cylinders.

When the brake pedal is operated the master cylinder piston applies a
force to the fluid, which, being virtually incompressible, causes the wheel
cylinder pistons to expand the brake shoes until they touch the brake

A   BRAKE PEDAL
B   MASTER CYLINDER
C   FLUID RESERVOIR
D   STOP LIGHT SWITCH
E   HYDRAULIC LINE
F   THREE-WAY CONNECTION
G   BRAKE HOSE BRACKET
H   BRAKE HOSE
J   WHEEL CYLINDER
K   HAND-BRAKE LEVER
L   BRAKE PUSH BAR
M   CABLE CONDUIT TUBE
N   FRONT WHEEL BRAKE
P   REAR WHEEL BRAKE

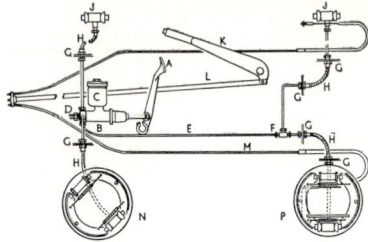

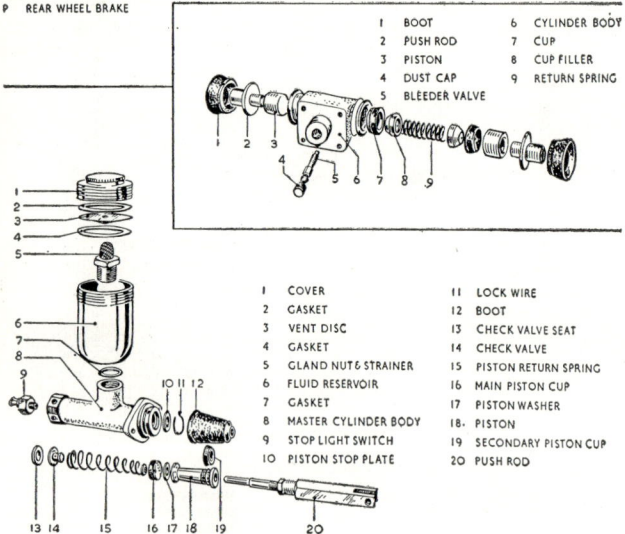

1   BOOT   6   CYLINDER BODY
2   PUSH ROD   7   CUP
3   PISTON   8   CUP FILLER
4   DUST CAP   9   RETURN SPRING
5   BLEEDER VALVE

1   COVER   11 LOCK WIRE
2   GASKET   12 BOOT
3   VENT DISC   13 CHECK VALVE SEAT
4   GASKET   14 CHECK VALVE
5   GLAND NUT & STRAINER   15 PISTON RETURN SPRING
6   FLUID RESERVOIR   16 MAIN PISTON CUP
7   GASKET   17 PISTON WASHER
8   MASTER CYLINDER BODY   18 PISTON
9   STOP LIGHT SWITCH   19 SECONDARY PISTON CUP
10 PISTON STOP PLATE   20 PUSH ROD

FIG. 42. A LATER VERSION OF THE HYDRAULIC BRAKING SYSTEM
(*Centre*) A typical wheel cylinder. (*Below*) A master cylinder

drums. This limits the amount of pedal travel and further effort on the
pedal increases the force applied to the brake shoes. The pressure gener-
ated in the master cylinder is transmitted equally and without loss to the
pistons of each wheel cylinder so that the forces applied to the various
shoes are identical and balanced braking is obtained.

When the pressure on the foot pedal is released the brake shoe pull-off springs force the wheel cylinder pistons back and the fluid passes back to the master cylinder, ready for the next application of the brakes.

When disc brakes are fitted to the front wheels, the principle is the same, except that the operating cylinders are housed in callipers which straddle the discs, so that the opposed pistons force two brake pads, which are faced with friction material, against the sides of each disc.

The hydraulic system of the 411 range is duplicated, the front and rear brakes having separate circuits, so that if, say, a rear-brake pipeline should leak, the front brakes will still remain effective. If a dual-circuit brake warning lamp is fitted (an optional extra, mounted between the two main instruments), failure of one brake circuit will be indicated by the lamp lighting-up. The bulb should be checked from time to time by pressing the lens inwards while the ignition is switched on.

Routine Maintenance. One of the main features of hydraulic brakes is that routine attention is reduced to a minimum, being confined primarily to checking, at 1,500-mile intervals, the fluid level in the supply tank, which should be topped up to within $\frac{1}{2}$ in. below the base of the reservoir filler neck with genuine Lockheed brake fluid. The supply tank should not be filled completely.

Insufficient fluid in the reservoir can result in air entering the brake operating system, causing a "spongy" feel when the brake pedal is depressed.

On the 411 range of vehicles fitted with manual transmission, the brake fluid reservoir is divided into three compartments, one for each brake circuit and one for the hydraulically-operated clutch. On automatic-transmission vehicles no clutch fluid reservoir is needed, as the drive is provided by a torque converter.

The brake (and clutch) fluid level can be seen through the translucent plastic reservoir. It should be level with the upper ledge of the reservoir.

Topping-up should be necessary only at long intervals. A rapid or considerable fall in the fluid level indicates either over-filling, or a leak at some point in the system, which should be traced and rectified.

To check for leaks, an assistant should be asked to pump the brake pedal once or twice and then hold it down firmly while you examine each pipeline connexion.

Two points to watch are first, that the steel pipes at the rear of the car sometimes develop pin-hole leaks due to rusting, causing loss of fluid which could be dangerous if the trouble were not spotted in time; and secondly, on the 1200 models the handbrake cables can chafe against the rear suspension arms and often wear through at this point. Protective plastic sleeves were fitted as a modification on later models, but if your car is unmodified, a short length of small-diameter rubber hose, split so that it can be slipped over the cable and secured by a couple of turns of wire at each end, will solve the problem.

Brake Adjustment. When pedal travel becomes excessive the brake shoes must be adjusted to compensate for wear of the brake linings. When disc brakes are fitted to the front axle, only the drum brakes on the rear wheels will require adjustment. The pistons which operate the friction pads in the front brakes are self-adjusting.

Before beginning work, first make sure that the tyres are inflated to the correct pressure and that the front wheel bearings have no excessive bearing "play."

Jack up the car to allow each wheel to be adjusted in turn and ensure that the wheel rotates freely. The handbrake, of course, should be in the fully-released position when adjusting the rear brakes, at least one other wheel being securely checked to prevent movement.

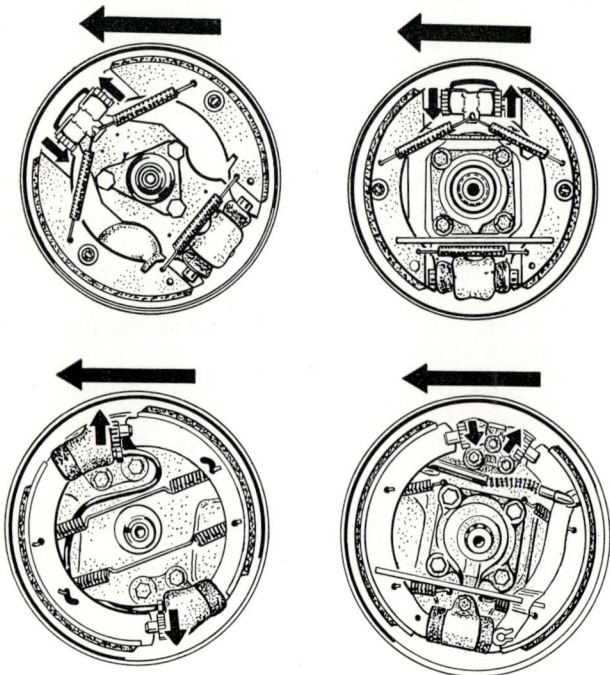

FIG. 43. BRAKE ADJUSTMENT

The larger arrows show the direction of travel of the wheel while the smaller arrows show the correct direction in which to rotate the adjusters. (*Upper drawings*) Typical assemblies on a private car. (*Lower drawings*) Brakes on Transporter

On all models except the 1600, holes are provided in the wheels and brake drums through which a screwdriver may be passed to rotate the adjusters. A torch is useful to enable the position of the adjusters to be located without difficulty, or a mirror may be used to reflect light through the hole into the drum.

There are two toothed adjusters on each brake, enabling the two brake shoes to be adjusted individually. Spin the wheel and, with a screwdriver, lever the adjusters round in opposite directions, as shown in Fig. 43, until the wheel is locked on the drum, and then slacken back each adjuster three to four teeth until the wheel rotates freely. This adjustment should be done with the brake drums cold.

The arrangements shown in Fig. 43 are typical of the various models but the backplates on some cars have been, in effect, rotated in respect to the axle so that the adjusters appear at different positions from those shown. Nevertheless the direction in which the adjusting wheels must be turned remains the same.

The only "odd man out" is the 1600 model, on which the brakes are not adjusted through the brake drums, but through holes in the brake backplate. Otherwise the method of adjustment is the same.

The brakes should now be tested on the road. A good stretch of dry surface, preferably uncambered, should be selected for the purpose. The brakes should be applied hard at about 30 m.p.h. and the braking marks should be examined to determine whether any wheel is locking before the remainder. It should also be noted whether there is a tendency to pull towards one side of the road.

If it is found that the brakes are inefficient or unbalanced, the cause is most probably grease on the linings. It is extremely important that the linings should be kept free from grease and oil. The use of correct front-wheel bearing lubricant and care not to overfill the transmission, as well as replacing grease retainers when leakage is indicated, will help to maintain braking efficiency. If the linings are badly saturated with grease or oil, new, relined brake shoes should be fitted.

Bleeding the Brakes. As mentioned above, insufficient fluid in the reservoir can result in air entering the system and making the brakes feel "spongy." If this condition is suspected, it will be necessary to bleed the air from the hydraulic system and your authorized dealer should be consulted. If such service is not readily available, however, the reservoir should be filled with the correct fluid and maintained at least half-full throughout the operation. Otherwise, air may be drawn in, necessitating a fresh start.

Remove the rubber cap and attach a rubber tube to the bleeder screw on one of the wheel cylinders, allowing the free end of the tube to be submerged in a little fluid in a clean glass jar. Open the bleeder screw one complete turn. The brake pedal should be depressed slowly and allowed to return unassisted. This pumping action should be repeated with a slight pause between each operation. A watch should be kept on the flow of liquid in the jar and when air bubbles cease to appear, the pedal should be held down firmly and the bleeder screw securely tightened. Repeat this operation on all wheel cylinders.

Clean fluid that has been bled from the system should be allowed to stand for several hours to allow the air contained   it to disperse, before the fluid is again used. Dirty or discoloured fluid, if not contaminated by

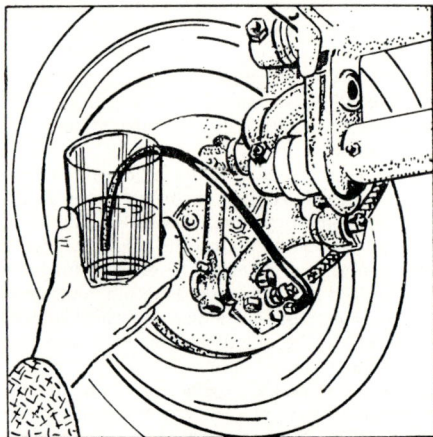

FIG. 44. BLEEDING THE BRAKES

mineral oil or other fluids, may be filtered and used again. The safest plan, however, is to use fresh fluid.

The fluid in the system may become thick or gummy after about two years in service or after a vehicle has been laid up for some considerable time, the system should be drained, flushed and refilled. To do this, pump all fluid out of the system through the bleeder screw of each wheel cylinder in turn as described above. All the fluid extracted should be discarded. Fill the reservoir with methylated spirit and flush the system by pumping as before. The supply tank should be replenished until at least a quart of spirit has passed through each wheel cylinder. Remove the supply tank and pour off any remaining spirit. Now refill with clean brake fluid and "bleed" the system.

If, however, the fluid has been contaminated by the use of mineral oil this flushing process may not prove effective. In this case the various units, including the pipelines, should be dismantled and thoroughly cleaned and all rubber parts, including flexible hoses, should be replaced.

The presence of mineral oil can be detected by examination of the cups and seals, which, if contaminated, will seem "dead" or lifeless to the touch. In more extreme cases the cups will swell by a visible amount and become distorted. If an oil has been used, this will frequently separate out when the fluid is allowed to stand in a glass jar; the layers of different fluid can readily be seen. The contaminated fluid should be disposed of immediately to avoid it being re-used accidentally.

Servicing the Hydraulic Braking System. Owners are advised to entrust this work to an authorized agent. However, if it is essential that the owner should carry out this work himself, the parts should be handled and assembled only under conditions of scrupulous cleanliness. A study of the individual units will show the order in which the parts should be dismantled and reassembled. The worst of the mud and grease should be cleaned off before any unit is removed. It is advisable to dismantle each individual unit on a bench covered with a sheet of clean paper.

The internal parts, particularly the rubbers, should not be handled with dirty hands. The partially-assembled units should not be swilled in petrol, paraffin or trichlorethylene as this will ruin the rubber cups and seals and give a misleading impression of their condition. Only brake fluid should be used to clean the rubber parts.

The rubber parts should be dried with a clean, fluff-free cloth and examined carefully for signs of damage, wear or distortion. If there is any doubt as to their condition they should be renewed. The cost is small in relation to the safety factor conferred by new parts. All the internal parts should be soaked in clean brake fluid for some hours before they are fitted and should be assembled wet. Care should be taken not to damage or turn back the lips of the rubber cups.

The master cylinder assembly consists of a housing with a highly-finished bore, into which are assembled the parts in the opposite sequence to dismantling.

Rear Brakes. The rear brakes differ from the front in that they have one trailing shoe and one leading shoe in each drum, the shoes being operated hydraulically by a single cylinder. Mechanical operation by the handbrake is provided by a simple mechanical expander.

Flexible Hoses. In some cases the cause of faulty brakes may be traced to a choked flexible hose. No attempt should be made to clear the obstruction by passing a wire through the hose as this will only result in damage to the hose. In view of the vital importance of the brakes, a new hose—or a set of new hoses—should be fitted if there is the slightest doubt about the condition of those in service.

Failure or blockage of a flexible hose is usually caused by the use of mineral oil or unsuitable fluid, or by a very long period of service.

A hose should never be subjected to any twisting strain. The correct method of installing a hose is first to attach the appropriate end to the wheel cylinder and then to fit the shake-proof washer and tighten the union nut while holding the hose union securely with a second spanner.

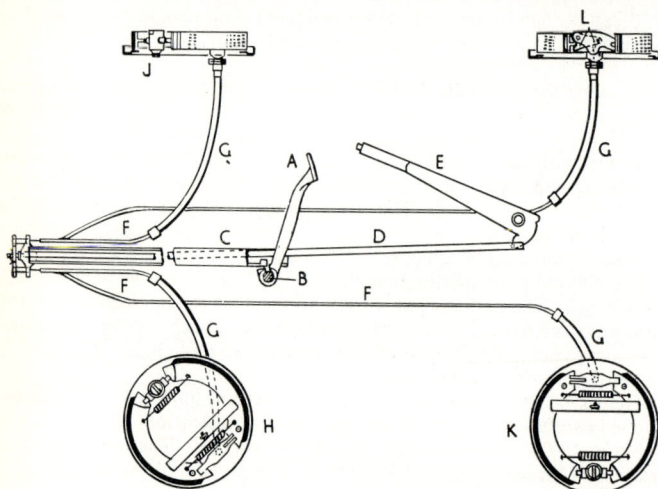

FIG. 45. LAYOUT OF MECHANICAL BRAKING SYSTEM

A. Brake pedal
B. Brake pedal shaft
C. Footbrake push bar
D. Handbrake push bar
E. Handbrake lever
F. Brake-cable conduit
G. Flexible metal tube
H. Front wheel brake
J. Adjusting device
K. Rear wheel brake
L. Brake-shoe expander

A periodic check of the hydraulic system can be carried out by adjusting the brake shoes until they are hard on the drums. The brake pedal should then be pumped hard once or twice and heavy pressure maintained for a minute or two. If the pedal withstands this pressure it can be assumed, as a rough check, that the hydraulic system is in order and free from leaks.

Fitting Replacement Shoes or Disc Brake Pads. Eventually it will be necessary to fit replacement brake shoes, which can be obtained from a VW dealer, the shoes on which the friction linings are worn-out being handed in in exchange. This is much more satisfactory than to attempt to reline the existing shoes, and the exchange system also operates for the disc-brake friction pads when disc brakes are fitted to the front wheels.

The condition of the brake linings can be inspected through openings in the brake drums. When disc brakes are fitted, the thickness of the lining remaining on the pads can be inspected with equal ease. The shoes or pads should be renewed when the thickness of the lining is reduced to $\frac{1}{8}$ in.

Renewing either the brake shoes or the disc brake pads is a straightforward mechanical job for the experienced owner but the novice would be well advised first to have a word with his VW dealer, in order to avoid any possible snags. In any event, it is advisable to check the seals in the brake operating pistons when the new brake shoes are fitted and also to make sure that the pistons of disc brakes are not binding in the calipers, owing to the presence of rust or grit. This emphasizes the fact that it is always advisable for the beginner to enlist expert assistance when dealing with such vital components as those in the braking system.

Adjusting the Handbrake (Hydraulic Braking System). In order to provide an independent braking system which will be effective in the unlikely event of the hydraulic system failing, the handbrake operates a mechanical leverage in each rear brake through enclosed flexible cables.

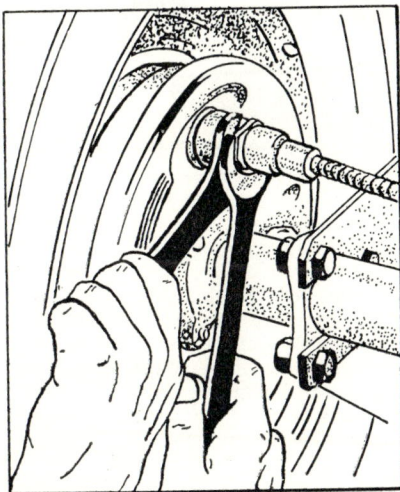

FIG. 46. ADJUSTING A MECHANICAL BRAKE

The adjusters for the cables are located just above the base of the handbrake lever. Up to August, 1955, the adjusting nuts at the forward end of the handbrake cables are enclosed by a removable cover between the front upper and lower suspension tubes. From August, 1955, onwards, however, modified brake cables were fitted. These are attached directly to the handbrake lever by adjustable nuts. If new cables are to be fitted, care should be taken to order the correct parts, since the earlier and later cables are of different lengths.

In order to carry out the adjustment, the rear wheels should be jacked up and the rubber cover that encloses the base of the handbrake lever on

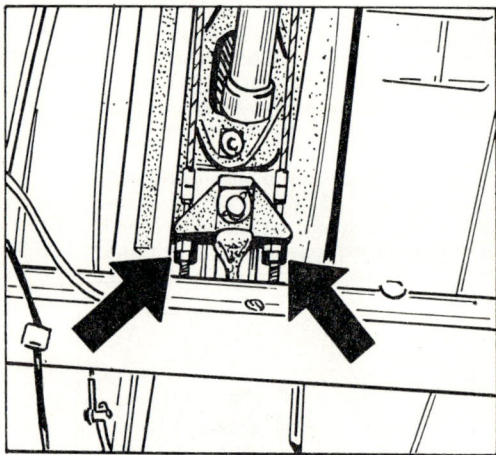

FIG. 47. HANDBRAKE ADJUSTMENT ON THE EARLIER TRANSPORTER

later models should be folded back, after sliding off the rubber ring, or unclipped and slid along the lever, in order to reveal the adjusting screws and locknuts. Alternatively, on earlier models the cover over the adjusting screws should be removed. The locknuts should then be slackened and each adjustment tightened up with a screwdriver until the wheels are just free to turn, making allowance, of course, for the drag of the differential pinions. The handbrake lever should then be pulled upward by two notches and the resistance at each wheel should be checked to ensure that the brakes are evenly balanced. With the handbrake at the fourth notch it should be impossible to turn the wheels by hand.

Mechanical Braking System. The mechanical braking system that is fitted to the standard model operates the foot and handbrakes through mechanical linkage at each wheel, the movement of the foot pedal or handbrake being transmitted through four cables that pass through conduits within the tubular backbone of the chassis.

Adjusting Mechanical Brakes. Much that has already been said concerning brake adjustment on the hydraulic braking system applies equally to the mechanical system. The method of adjustment is, however, different.

Adjustment is carried out at the rear of each brake back-plate. Preferably all four wheels should be jacked up clear of the ground. The handbrake lever should be released. Above the axle on each back-plate is a large brake-cable adjusting sleeve, secured by a lock-nut. The latter should be slackened and the cable adjusting nut turned clockwise, towards the back-plate.

Below the axle is a small hexagonal adjusting nut which should be tightened until the wheel can no longer be turned by hand. The brake-cable adjusting sleeve should then be slackened back until there is a very slight clearance between the end-fitting on the cable conduit and the adjusting sleeve. The lock-nut should now be tightened.

Finally, the brake-shoe adjusting nut should be slackened back until the brake drum can just rotate freely. A light tap on the head of the nut will position the adjusting cone correctly.

After carrying out the adjustment in the same manner on the remaining brakes, the handbrake should be pulled on by two notches and the resistance at each wheel should be checked. If there is any marked difference in drag, the brake-shoe adjusting nut on the wheel that has the greatest braking effect should be slackened back one flat at a time. When the handbrake is pulled on by four notches, it should not be possible to rotate the wheels by hand.

A road test should now be made as described earlier and any slight balancing of the brakes that may be necessary should be carried out by rotating only the brake-shoe adjusting nuts. The brake-cable adjusters should not be altered. Remember that the golden rule is to slacken-off slightly the adjustment on any wheel that locks before the remainder. Do not be tempted to tighten-up the other brakes, as there will be a risk of them binding in normal use.

Servicing the Mechanical System. Normally a complete overhaul of the braking system should be left to your VW dealer. It is, however, a fairly straightforward job to fit replacement brake shoes after the brake drums have been removed with the aid of a hub withdrawal tool. Dismantling is quite straightforward, it being necessary only to remove the expander and operating link and the leaf spring that bears on the brake shoes. The shoes can then be swung downwards and withdrawn from the locating pins.

When reassembling the shoes, new pull-off springs should be fitted (the springs are installed on the outsides of the shoes). The locating pins should be greased and their oblique ends should be towards the adjuster cones. The spring-loaded retaining pins must bed in the recesses in the reinforcement plate and the points of the leaf spring should be lightly greased. The operating link and expander should be fitted with the pin towards the front on the rear-wheel brakes and towards the rear on the front-wheel brakes.

The wheel bearings must be lubricated and the front hubs adjusted as described in Chapter 8, before any attempt is made to adjust and balance the brakes.

8 Suspension, Steering and Tyres

A NUMBER of items on the car may influence each other to a greater degree than is generally realized; for example, poor steering may not be due entirely to steering gear defects but can also be caused by incorrect wheel alignment, or incorrect tyre pressures and dragging brakes. Again, rapid wear of the tyres may be due to incorrect wheel alignment and dragging brakes or distorted brake drums. Numerous examples of the relationship between the tyres and other components will also be evident throughout this chapter. Under-inflated rear tyres, for example, will cause the car to wander; increasing the pressure of the rear tyres to the correct figure will often cure this symptom without any attention whatever to the steering gear.

A point which should be borne in mind by a driver new to the Volkswagen is the tendency of earlier models to "oversteer," owing to the use of a rear engine and independent rear suspension. This means that if a corner is entered fast, the rear of the car tends to swing outwards, calling for some reduction in the amount of steering lock which is applied. This characteristic gives delightfully light and responsive steering but, on the other hand, calls for some discretion when the roads are wet or icy. Many experienced drivers prefer to run with the rear tyres at the pressures recommended for full load (*see* Chapter 1) even when no passengers are being carried, as this minimizes the effect.

In particular, it is not advisable to arrive at a corner at too high a speed when the road surface is treacherous, as sudden closing of the throttle or application of the brakes may put the car into a slide.

From August, 1959, onwards, export models were fitted with a stabilizer bar which can also be installed on earlier vehicles. The enthusiastic owner will find this a worthwhile conversion as it considerably improves steering and roadholding. From March, 1960, onwards cars were fitted with hydraulic steering dampers—again a modification which might be worth discussing with the local VW agent. Enthusiasts can also obtain advice from the Speedwell Centre, 260–300 Berkhamsted Rd. Chesham, Bucks This firm produces a wide range of well-tested modifications for the VW which are marketed through a large European sales organization and also in the U.S.A. through Engineered Motor Products Inc. (better known to VW fans as EMPI). The Speedwell-Empi camber compensator greatly improves the roadholding and steering and is easily fitted by the do-it-yourself owner, the average time required being less than thirty minutes.

SUSPENSION

On all models except the 411, 411L, 411E and 411LE, the front suspension consists of two tubes, the outer ends of which carry pivoted, trailing torsion arms which are attached to torsion bars housed within the tubes. On earlier models the bars are built up from laminated springs and each is anchored at the centre so that road shocks are absorbed by the torsion or twisting of the bars. The torsion arms are connected by links carrying the stub axles, which swivel on king pins in the conventional manner. A steering damper is fitted between the upper end of the stub axle and the

FIG. 48. THE POWER UNIT AND REVISED REAR SUSPENSION OF THE 411 AND
411E MODELS

torsion arm link. Double-acting, telescopic hydraulic shock absorbers damp-out road shocks.

On the 1500 and 1500S models, an improved front suspension layout is fitted, round-section torsion bars being used instead of laminated torsion springs. This suspension is also used on the 1600 and on the 1200A and 1300 models and a stabilizing anti-roll bar is also fitted to the front suspension of this later range of cars.

On the 411, 411L, 411E and 411LE, Volkswagen broke new ground by using a T-shaped front sub-frame which supports the lower track-control arms and radius rods of the Macpherson-strut suspension system, in which the weight of the car is carried by a combined hydraulic damper and coil-spring suspension unit on each side, which incorporates a shock-absorber in the tubular strut. Since the stub-axles which carry the wheels are attached to the lower ends of the suspension units, each unit must swivel as the wheel is turned from lock to lock. Provision is made for this by ball joints at the base of each strut and by a combined swivel and thrust race at the upper end.

At the rear of the car the wheels are also independently sprung. Earlier models use swinging axle shafts with trailing arms, controlled by a torsion bar on each side which passes transversely across the car and is protected by a tube. When semi-automatic or automatic transmission was fitted, however, double-jointed axle shafts were used and this system was standard-ized on manual-transmission cars from 1969 onwards, since it gives better roadholding and steering than the simple swing-axle layout. It was further refined on the 411, 411L, 411E and 411LE by using semi-trailing wish-bones, a coil spring on each side and a telescopic shock-absorber inside each spring. Since a unitary-construction bodyshell is used for these cars, the rear suspension, engine and drive assembly is carried on a separate sub-frame which is bolted to the body.

The front suspension normally requires little maintenance, other than regular lubrication at the intervals specified in Chapter 1 and shown in the lubrication chart (no lubrication is required for the 411 range). If, how-ever, the car is mainly used on rough roads or if it is not driven more than about 600 miles per month, it is advisable to lubricate the points shown on the chart for earlier models every 800 miles, the torsion armlinks and the outer track rod joints being particularly important in this respect.

Adjusting Torsion Arm Link Pins. At regular intervals the torsion arm link pins should be checked by raising the car and rocking each front wheel by hand to check whether any end-play exists between the torsion arm link and the torsion arms themselves. If excessive play can be detected, the link pins should be adjusted. As it is essential to check the camber and the toe-in of the front wheels, calling for use of accurate equipment, the whole job is best left to a VW dealer, except in emergency.

The Shock Absorbers. The double-acting hydraulic shock absorbers fitted all models except the 411 range are of the sealed type and normally need no maintenance or topping-up. As the compression and rebound characteristics of the shock absorber are tuned to the suspension of the car, no attempt should be made to alter the adjustment or to fit different types of shock absorber. Nor should the front and rear shock absorbers be interchanged. The front shock absorbers are painted black, the rear units are red-brown and those for the front axle of the Transporter, grey.

If the damping action appears to be insufficient, it is not a difficult matter to remove the shock absorbers and to test them by holding them vertically and compressing them by hand. This will, of course, only indicate whether or not there is any resistance; it will not determine the efficiency of the compression and the rebound strokes. The only satis-factory method of dealing with a defective shock absorber is to fit a re-placement of the same type.

It should be remembered, however, that apparent shock absorber failure or inefficiency is often due to nothing more serious than deterioration of the rubber bearings. A VW dealer possesses the tools required to press fresh bushes into the shock absorber eyes.

FRONT WHEEL BEARINGS

Testing Wheel Bearings. Occasionally the front wheels should be jacked up and the bearings should be tested by grasping the tyre at the top and bottom and rocking the wheel vertically about the hub. Do not confuse any possible looseness which may exist in the various steering connexions with wheel-bearing play; watch for relative movement between the brake drum and the brake back-plate.

FIG. 49. THE MACPHERSON-STRUT FRONT SUSPENSION SYSTEM AND THE STEERING GEAR OF THE 411 AND 411E RANGE

If it has been determined that excessive play exists in the front-wheel bearings these should be adjusted. After removing the grease cap and bending back the tabs of the locking washer, slacken the lock-nut and tighten the hub-adjusting nut while the wheel is rotating, until a heavy drag can just be felt. Now turn back the adjusting nut until the wheel is perfectly free but without perceptible end-float. It should just be possible to slide the thrust washer, fitted beneath the adjusting nut, sideways with a screwdriver. Check the adjustment again after the locking nut has been tightened. Tap the tabs of the locking washer into place. If they break off in the process, it will be necessary to fit a new washer and to carry out the adjustment again. Clean the grease cap and refill it with wheel-bearing grease.

Once a year the hub bearings should be removed, washed in paraffin and repacked with wheel-bearing grease. For this job special bearing-extracting and installing tools are needed.

Cleanliness is most essential when dealing with all types of bearings. The car should never be run with the grease caps missing since this would allow an easy entry for grit and other road dirt. The front hub grease retainer should be renewed if necessary.

THE STEERING GEAR

The worm-and-sector steering box is bolted to the upper front axle tube and the steering column operates the worm shaft through a flexible coupling.

Inside the box, the shaft carries a helical thread which, when the shaft is turned, imparts a backward or forward motion to a spherical sector carried in a rocker shaft. Movement is thus transmitted through the rocker shaft to the steering drop-arm below the box.

Adjusting Steering Gear. Adjustments are provided on earlier models to eliminate end-play on the sector shaft, which also takes up backlash between the worm and the sector, and for end-float of the worm shaft. It

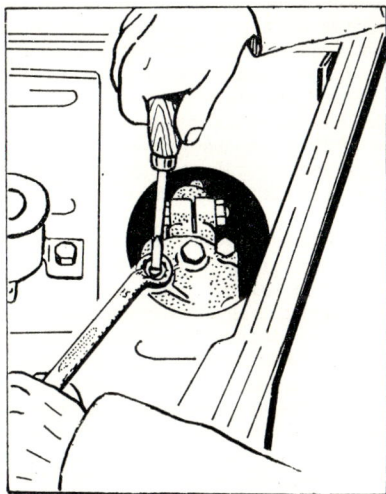

Fig 50. Adjusting Steering Sector

is necessary to carry out these adjustments very carefully and as the work calls for some experience, it is better to leave it to a VW agent and this should certainly be done in the case of the high-efficiency steering gearbox fitted to the 1200A, 1300, 1500, 1600 and 411 models.

When it is necessary for the owner to carry out the job on the earlier 1200 models, however, the front end of the car should be jacked up so that the wheels are clear of the ground. The lock-nut on the sector-shaft adjusting screw shown in Fig. 50 and the clamping bolt that locks the worm shaft bearing adjusting sleeve should be slackened.

Any play in the worm shaft should then be taken up by turning the adjusting sleeve clockwise. This adjustment should not be overdone as there is a risk of damaging the worm thrust bearings. The sector shaft end-play can then be dealt with by tightening the adjusting screw as far as it will go and slackening it back by one-eighth of a turn.

After tightening up the lock-nut and clamping bolt, the steering should be tested by turning the wheels from lock to lock. There should be no perceptible tight spot at any point. If, however, the steering is stiff after the adjustment has been correctly made, it will be necessary to remove the steering box in order to dismantle it and renew any defective parts. This, again, is a job for a VW dealer or agent.

Checking the Steering Geometry. Satisfactory steering depends not only on the condition of the steering gearbox and connexions, but also on the maintenance of the correct steering angles and geometry of the whole of the front suspension and steering assembly. For example, if these angles are upset as a result of a minor kerb collision, the steering will be adversely affected and tyre wear may be greatly increased. Because the steering angles are determined by the initial assembly of the parts, accurate checking of the adjustment of these angles is beyond the scope of the owner. If the steering is unsatisfactory or tyre wear is rapid, the car should be taken to an authorized VW agent for expert attention.

Tyre and Wheel Balance. Provided that the steering gearbox is kept topped up with the correct grade of oil and tyre pressures are maintained at the correct figures, the steering should remain satisfactory for many thousands of miles. In fact, as already suggested, symptoms such as wheel wobble, a tendency to wander and heavy steering, can often be traced to such faults as uneven or incorrect tyre pressures, unbalanced wheels and tyres, uneven tyre wear, or weak shock absorbers or springs. The steering geometry and the correct toe-in of the front wheels are also vital factors.

On the Volkswagen, as with most other modern cars, a compromise between lightness of steering and steering stability has been arrived at which makes tyre balance of extreme importance. The faster the car is driven, the more vital does this become.

The assembly of wheel and tyre should not be out of balance to an extent exceeding 1 oz. at the rim of the wheel. In cases where the wheel assembly is out of balance to an amount exceeding this figure it must be balanced by using special equipment that checks not only the static but also dynamic balance. Static unbalance causes vertical movement of the wheel (or "tramp") while dynamic unbalance causes wheel-wobble or "shimmy."

THE TYRES

Apart from unbalanced wheels or incorrect steering geometry and wheel alignment, the most usual cause of excessive tyre wear is under-inflation of the tyres. Although some increase in comfort can be obtained by running the tyres at lower than the recommended pressures, this can be done only at the expense of tyre wear and also results in deterioration in roadholding and braking.

When the pressure is too low, undue bending and flexing of the tyre walls occurs. In addition, the tread becomes worn on the outer edges, while the centre remains comparatively unworn. The rate of tread wear is consequently increased, owing to the fact that wear is not distributed evenly over the whole of the tread.

Excessive flexing of the tyre walls can also build up high temperatures owing to the friction between the plies, shortening the life of the tyre and creating the risk of a blow-out. It is for this reason that higher pressures than normal are recommended for cross-ply tyres when there is a prospect of long periods of driving at high speed, or if the vehicle is heavily loaded. As a general guide, increase the pressures by 3–4 lb/sq in. (0·2–0·3 kg/sq cm). Owing to their construction, radial-ply tyres do not normally require increased pressures for fast driving.

The necessity for checking the tyre pressures at regular intervals will be appreciated when it is understood that every normal inner tube, even when new, loses pressure at the rate of from 1 to 3 lb per week, owing to a process known as "diffusion." Oxygen from the air in the tube is absorbed by the rubber and a corresponding amount of oxygen is given off from the outer surface of the tube. It is necessary, therefore, to restore this slight loss of pressure even when the tubes are in first-class condition.

An advantage of tubeless tyres, to which reference is made below, is that they are not subject to this diffusion, since the casings are much thicker than a conventional inner tube. Alternatively, synthetic rubber tubes can be obtained which do not lose pressure in this manner.

Jacking-up the Car. On early models a screw-type jack is provided which is operated by applying the sparking plug box spanner to the hexagon at the top of the jack. On later models, the type of jack shown in Fig. 51 is provided. With this type, the handle should be inserted in the socket in the operating arm and moved backwards and forwards, as shown in Fig. 51, to raise the car. To lower the car, transfer the handle to the hole on the rear flange of the jack, as also shown in Fig. 51, and apply light downward pressure. The pillar of the jack can be pressed downwards until it is in contact with the ground but can be raised only if light pressure is applied to the operating handle just as described.

Both types of jack engage with a square socket beneath each side of the car, just in front of the rear wheel. Make sure, before jacking up, that the car is level and that at least one wheel on the side that is not to be raised is blocked securely. Also, if the car is close to a kerb, allow sufficient

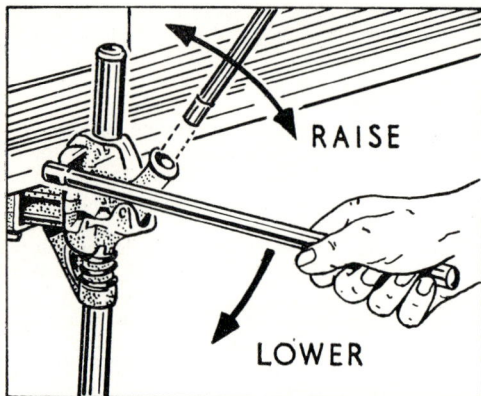

FIG. 51. THE JACK USED ON LATER MODELS

On early cars a screw jack was provided which was operated by the box spanner used for the sparking plugs and wheel bolts

space for the wheel to be withdrawn when the retaining bolts have been unscrewed.

Mention of the bolts raises another point. When refitting the wheel, it will be necessary to insert one bolt and to tighten this sufficiently to allow the wheel to be swung round until its bolt holes line up with the remaining holes in the brake drum. The other retaining bolts can then be inserted.

One further point for the benefit of the novice: the initial slackening and final tightening of the wheel bolts should always be done before the wheel is raised from the ground, to avoid rocking the car while it is jacked up. In the case of the front wheels, of course, this will in any case be necessary owing to the fact that the handbrake acts only on the rear wheels.

Repairing Tyres and Tubes. Most owners will be familiar with the usual method of removing outer covers and repairing inner tubes. In the restricted space available in this chapter, therefore, it is proposed to discuss only the less-familiar technique that must be used with tubeless tyres. It may be mentioned that when the time comes to renew the tyres on your car or van, tubeless tyres can be fitted either singly, in pairs or as a set. They have a number of advantages and, since their cost is no higher than a standard cover and inner tube, owners may consider the conversion worthwhile.

Tubeless Tyres. In the tubeless tyre the inner tube is replaced by a special rubber lining which forms part of the outer cover itself and the construction of the tyre bead is modified to make an effective air seal between tyre and rim. The valve is of a normal type but is mounted directly on the wheel rim.

Tubeless tyres are not, of course, puncture-proof but a nail or other sharp object which pierces the casing does not allow air to escape. The unstretched rubber inner lining grips the intruder closely and forms a seal around it. The nail can, therefore, be left in the tyre until it is convenient to have the tyre repaired; the puncture, in fact, may not be discovered until the tyre is examined, as it should be periodically. It is safe to run a tubeless tyre that has been punctured in this manner for 1,000 miles or more.

The only disadvantage of tubeless tyres from the owner's point of view is that unless a garage airline is available, it is difficult to obtain the initial seal between the beads of the tyre and the flanges of the rim. The garage method is to remove the centre from the valve and apply the airline so that the rush of air springs the beads of the tyre against the rim, providing a satisfactory seal. The valve core is then replaced and the tyre inflated in the normal manner. It will be obvious that if an owner attempts to expand a tyre by using only a hand-pump or foot-pump there will be an insufficient volume of air available to produce an effective seal.

Fortunately, as the tyre can be run at least a thousand miles with a nail or other puncturing implement imbedded in it, it should seldom be impossible to take the tyre to a garage for repair, even assuming that for some reason the spare wheel is out of action. Moreover, it is possible to repair all normal punctures, as described below, without deflating the tyre or removing it from the rim. It must be emphasized, however, that the pressure in the tyre should not be allowed to fall below 5 lb per sq in. unless a garage airline is available for re-inflation.

Repairing Punctures in Tubeless Tyres. A special repair kit can be obtained which allows a puncture to be repaired without removing the tyre from the rim. A tool rather like a bodkin is inserted through the puncture to free it from road grit and is then dipped in rubber solution and again inserted in the hole and withdrawn. The end of a short length of rubber of circular section is next gripped in the same tool, dipped in the solution and pushed through the tread, as shown in Fig. 52.

The tool is then withdrawn and the rubber plug cut off about $\frac{1}{8}$ in. (3 mm) from the surface of the tread. If a special repair kit is not avail-

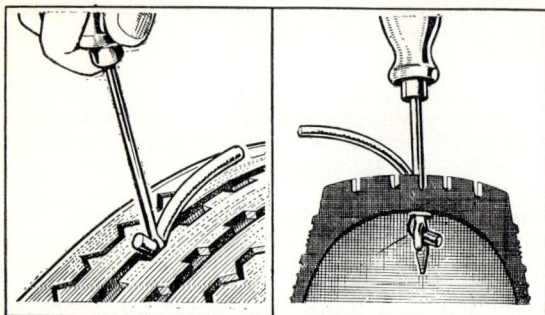

FIG. 52. REPAIRING TUBELESS TYRES
A short length of rubber plug is inserted with a special tool

able or if the damage is more serious, the tyre should be removed by a garage and an ordinary vulcanized repair made to the inner surface. *In any case, tyre manufacturers consider a rubber-plug repair to be a temporary measure only, until a vulcanized repair can be carried out.*

Radial-ply tyres should not be repaired by the use of plugs—assuming that they are of the tubeless type. In most cases, however, the use of an inner tube with radial-ply tyres is specified for Volkswagen models.

9 The bodywork

However conscientiously an owner may maintain and tune his car, the unhappy truth is that others tend to judge it largely by its general appearance! Appearance is also a vital factor—often a deciding one—when the time comes to sell the car.

Excellent cleaning and polishing preparations may be obtained from your Volkswagen dealer; alternatively, a choice may be made from the wide range stocked by accessory dealers and garages.

The finish on the body will retain its freshness for years, provided that it is kept clean. Deterioration is inevitable if the body is allowed to get very dirty. Fairly frequent cleaning is, in any case, a quicker and more satisfactory job than an occasional "spring-clean."

Grease and oil—and even tar if it is fresh—can be removed from the finish by using a solution of two-thirds petrol and one-third engine oil. If the tar is stubborn use a dry-cleaning fluid.

When the mud has been allowed to dry on, wash it off with plenty of cold water and a clean sponge. Finish with a leather. Use a good flow of water at low pressure from the hose; reserve the high-pressure jet for the wheels and undersides of the wings. If a hose is not available, a bucket of water containing a wash-wax shampoo works wonders—besides being a more comfortable method in cold weather!

For the first two months with a new car, however, while the paint is still hardening, it is better to use cold water only. Do not polish or wax the finish during this period.

The Tyres. Sponging with cold water is all that is necessary for normal cleaning of the tyres. Oil and grease should be removed with soap and water. Stains on the white portion of "white wall" tyres can be removed with a little domestic scouring powder and a stiff scrubbing brush. "Brillo" soap-filled wire-wool scouring pads are also very effective. *Petrol or paraffin must not be used for cleaning tyres as they cause rapid deterioration of the rubber.*

The appearance of the tyres can be improved by painting them with a suitable tyre paint, obtainable from most accessory dealers. Alternatively, try the effect of brushing in a proprietary grate polish and then lightly polishing it off with a brush. A marked improvement in appearance can be obtained in a few minutes at negligible cost.

Windows and Windscreen. Particular care should be taken not to scratch the glass. If it is cleaned at the same time as the rest of the car there is a possibility that particles of grit will cause fine scratches that can make night driving very unpleasant, since they reflect the street lighting and the lamps of approaching vehicles.

FIG. 53. THE DEVON CARAVETTE, ONE OF THE POPULAR CARAVAN CONVERSIONS OF THE MICROBUS OR KOMBI

Flush-off any heavy deposits on the glass when washing the bodywork, but leave the final cleaning and polishing until afterwards. Each glass should then be washed in turn, making sure that the water and the sponge are quite clean and free from grit. With all respect to petrol stations, it is not a good plan to encourage the attendant to wipe over the screen with a doubtfully-clean leather or cloth, however enthusiastic he may be!

If the glass is very dirty, a little household ammonia mixed with warm water will help enormously. Alternatively, a domestic window-cleaning preparation will give a good sparkle, but don't add glass-cleaning fluids to the washing water, as they may affect the paintwork. Clean linen cloth is best for polishing glass. Old linen cloth which has been washed is better than new material for this purpose as it is softer. Do not apply car polish to the glass as it tends to cause rain spots to smear in the track of the wiper arm.

Chromium. Generally a light rub with a clean, soft cloth will be all that is necessary to remove dust from the chromium-plated parts. However, if the chromium is covered with dead insects, tar spots or mud, it should be washed with warm soapy water and then cleaned with a non-abrasive liquid car polish. This polish should also be used if the chromium shows signs of tarnishing. Do not use ordinary metal polishes as they may contain abrasives which would ruin the plating. Rusty chrome may be restored by wiping on "Jenolite" rust-remover, allowing the preparation to act for five or ten minutes and then wiping it off. Finish off with wax polish.

Upholstery. The surface of *plastic upholstery* need only be wiped over occasionally with a damp cloth. If dirt has accumulated, use one of the special dry-foam upholstery cleaners that can be bought from garages and accessory shops. Care should be taken not to flood the upholstery with water. After this, the upholstery should be wiped dry and polished with a soft duster. Household cleaners, bleaching agents and dry-cleaning fluids must not be used on the upholstery.

Leather upholstery should be cleaned with a damp cloth and a little saddle soap. Do not use chemical cleaners or polishes on leather upholstery, owing to the risk of staining the surface.

Fabric Upholstery. If a vacuum cleaner is available, the upholstery will benefit from a weekly vacuuming to remove embedded dust. Otherwise, a brush or whisk broom should be used. Grease or oil stains on fabric upholstery can be removed by using a proprietary cleaning fluid. The fluid should not be poured directly on to the spot, as there is a risk of forming a ring. A clean cloth should be moistened with the fluid and rubbed lightly on the stain with a circular motion, starting outside the spot and working towards the centre. If this does not completely remove the mark, the remaining discoloration is probably due to the presence of dirt; cleaning agents normally remove only the grease. A light sponging with lukewarm suds should complete the treatment. An excessive amount of water should not be used owing to the risk of saturating the padding beneath the upholstery.

The Convertible Top. The folding top or hood on convertible models can easily be raised or lowered single-handed. The life of the hood, however, largely depends on the manner in which the fabric is stowed when in the folded position. The sequence below should be carefully followed.

To lower the hood, first pull downwards the two clamps on the windscreen, thus releasing the header rail and allowing the hood to be folded back. The outer cover should be pulled clear of the linkages on both sides to avoid it being trapped. The lining should also be pushed inwards clear of the linkages. Next, press the hood downwards until the spring-loaded catches on each side engage with the slots cut in the side rails. The caps of the clamps should then be placed over the header guides and the levers pressed down. The cover can now be placed over the hood from the rear, pulling it snugly into place. The ornamental strip along the top edge of the cover should be visible.

It is worth remembering that the rear-view mirror fitted to the convertible is adjustable to provide the ideal view, whether the hood is lowered or raised. When the hood is in the raised position, the rod carrying the mirror should be swung downwards and the mirror pushed towards the windscreen until the stop can be felt. This will bring the mirror into line with the rear window. When the hood is lowered, however, the mirror should be raised by pulling the bracket backwards until the stop can be felt and swinging the rod upwards.

Care of the Hood. The fabric of the convertible hood and the sunshine roof of the de luxe Microbus should always be dry before the hood is folded. If the car is driven on dusty roads, the hood should be lightly beaten once a week and the fabric brushed in line with the weave of the material; if sharp particles of grit become embedded in the fabric its life will be shortened.

Another possible source of damage is failure to secure the lowered hood tightly by means of the catches which engage with the slot cut in the side rail. If the hood is not firmly held, the catches should be screwed further into their retainers after loosening the lock-nuts, which should be tightened after the adjustment has been carried out.

Spots may be removed from the material by using an "art" gum eraser. Fuel or dry-cleaning agents should not be used since they cause deterioration of the rubber plies in the hood. The material should be washed only when it is very dirty, using castile or olive-oil-based soap, which should be worked up into thick suds. After scrubbing the material with a soft brush, the suds should be flushed off with clear water. No traces of soap should be allowed to remain on the material and suds should also be washed off the bodywork of the car.